Super Heroes
And Other
Drawings

THE ART OF MARTIN O DAGENAIS

MARTIN OLIVIER DAGENAIS
SUPER HEROES AND OTHER DRAWINGS

Forward

Perseverance, willpower, motivation... These are the easy answers you get when questioned about what it takes to achieve the level my little brother has reached with his drawings.

None of these terms apply to him. I know this for a fact. No. He's just pathologically stubborn.

When Martin showed me the first comic he drew (and wrote), it was about this guy who had a ninja star stuck in his eye. This was not a recent accident, no, it was a long-standing feature of the protagonist my brother cooked up. His wound bled constantly, because blood is cool, and blood was the only thing that was colored in the otherwise monochromatic vomit of a story that he had written because it also made the whole page cool-looking.

The guy's hairdo (actually, everyone's hairdos now that I think about it) could only be described as a love letter to Jon Bon Jovi's early career days. Once you got passed the fact that this guy's perma-wound and forever-lodged foreign body did not create a constant series of horrible infections, you had to question if the theoretical amount of hair spray needed to coif this bastard's head every morning could be considered ethical. The '80s were a rough time, and the ozone layer was serious business. I swear to the great spaghetti monster in the sky that I remember complaining about this.

The above description is not a flattering one, and trust me, this is the polite version. For instance, I did not mention his drawings were absolute "garbage" (read that word with French pronunciation, think "croissant". Say it with me – "gar-bag-je"). As his older brother, I believed it was my sacred duty to take a steaming dump onto his every effort should I find any kind of imperfection. Because that's the kind of brotherly love we dished out to each other.

But my brother is an incredibly stubborn person. Still is.

He kept drawing that trash comic. He kept showing them to me. There was no use telling him what I honestly thought, he just kept at it.

He never stopped. It was not a fad. In high school, he became known as the comic guy. In college, he got published in a few 'zines. In his adult life, he's been asked to participate in podcasts. People ask his "opinion" on things. I'm rolling my eyes as I'm writing this.

I sometimes regret telling him what I did back then. I was not wise enough to realize I was witnessing true passion for an art that would only get better with time. His latest drawings aren't just good, they are textbook examples of the many aspects budding artists are trying to master. Light and shadow, body proportions, dimensions, and angles.   You name it, he lives and breathes it.

A literal forest of paper was sacrificed to all might Kirby in the sky to reach this point. We should be thankful Martin switched to digital drawing it would be three forests by now. I can honestly say that my brother has reached a level of skill for which I have no words for. He's among the best of the best that I've seen, and I constantly show off what he does to strangers so that I can make them think I'm an interesting person.

So, what is all this about?

It's something along the lines that practice makes perfect, that failure is part of the learning process, and stubbornness is cool when you just want to do that thing you love.
I was fourteen when he showed me that comic. As of this writing, I'll be fifty in a few months. I still think, truly, honestly, that his first comic was absolute utter horse%@#!, but I'm wise enough now to know that it was a necessary step to drawing everything else that he has drawn ever since.
And now I'm being asked to write a forward for his first book? What, you need this by Monday? Hey, I told you I would not be too nice. This is the best I could come up with.
Okay, I'll be sappy but just this one. You embody the Dagenais motto. Like our dad and his dad before he used to say, "If it's worth being done, it needs to be done right".
Sincerely, your older brother.

Contact me:
Instagram: @martinodagenais
martinodagenias@gmail.com

Index

Forward I am vengeance
Drawing based on a photograph by @batmaninhouston
Page 8 Silver Surfer
Drawing based on the extraordinary art of Ysu Yeong Kim
Page 9 Snikt
Wolverine drawing based on a @xmstudios statue
Page 10 Killer Croc
Based on a statue by @prime1studio
Page 11 The Batman
Page 12 Spider-Man symbiote
Based on a statue by @unboxingbrosph
Page 13 The Hulk
Drawing based on the digital sculpture by artist John Newell
Page 14 Soundwave
Based on the bust from XM Studios
Page 15 Tron
Page 16 The Joker
Page 17 Moon night
Drawing based on a digital sculpture by artist @ygor.3d
Page 18 Black cat
Black CAT is based on the amazing cosplayer @enjinight she's a must follow
Page 19 Wolverine rage
Page 20 The Human Torch
The drawing is based on a bodybuilder named @max_true
Page 21 The Punisher
Art based on the digital sculpture of Bloodshot by @caleb_nefzen
Page 22 Electro
Based on a statue by @xmstudios
Page 23 The Silver Surfer reflection
Based on the sculpture by @j.vitor.art
Page 24 Mazinger Z
Based on a digital sculpture by the amazing artist @joshnizzi.art from @prime1studio
Page 25 Spawn
The drawing is based on a digital sculpture by artist Merlaub Art
Page 26 Teenage mutant ninja turtles
Drawing based on a digital sculpture by @tiagorios3
Page 27 Red Sonja
This drawing is based on a sculpture by the incredible artiste @renan_soarez3d.
Page 28 Cable
Drawing based on a statue from XM Studios
Page 29 Wolverine side view
Inspired by a ZBrush sculpture of an @benoliverart painting He's a must follow
Page 30 The Silver Surfer speed
Based on the sculpture by artist Franco Carlesimo
Page 31 Lion-O
Drawing based on the digital sculpture of @Luiz.alipio3d

Page 32 Hell Boy
The drawing is based on a digital sculpture from the amazing artist @raphalbero
Page 33 Daredevil blind jump
Based on a sculpture by Hard Hero
Page 34 Catwoman
Based on cosplay @kamiko_zero photo by @lieliseeva.photo
Page 35 Venom
Drawing based on a digital sculpture by @ozaniart
Page 36 Power Girl
Based on a @prime1studio statue
Page 37 Thor
Based on a sculpture by @raphalbero
Page 38 Deadpool
Drawing based on a digital sculpture by the amazing artist @eduardosilva3dart
Page 39 Optimus Prime
Based on the statue by SOSKILL
Page 40 The Laughing Batman
Drawing based on the amazing digital sculpture by @rafagrassetti
Page 41 Wolverine bust
Inspired by the sculpture of artist Daniel Bel
Page 42 Nightwing
Based on the extraordinary cosplayer @masked_mateo
Page 43 Creature from the Black Lagoon
Page 44 Ming-Na the Book of Boba Fett
Page 45 Boba Fett
Page 46 Ghost rider
Page 47 The Wolverine concept art.
Commission for @namesakestudios
Page 48 Cyclops
The drawing is based on the @xmstudios statue made by the amazing artist @rafamustaine
Page 49 Spider-Man Noir
Based on the concept art of Jayson Fitch
Page 50 Zombie
The drawing is based on the sculpture by artist Dominic Qwek
Page 51 Spawn bust
Based on a digital sculpture by Yosuke Ishikawa
Page 52 The Batcave
Drawing based on a statue by @prime1studio
Page 53 The Black Panther
Based on the @sideshow statue
Page 54 Macross
Page 55 Civil War
Page 56 Bane
The drawing is based on a bust from PRIME 1 STUDIO
Page 57 Ant-Man
The drawing is based on a statue from XM Studios
Page 58 Logan
The drawing is based on a photo by @yole47 You guys have to check out his profile, he is not just a collector but an incredible photographer.

Page 59 Cyclops dark
The drawing is based on a statue from XM Studios
Page 60 The Joker surgeon
Sketch-based on @mikemayhewstudio JOKER/HARLEY: criminal sanity #4 variant cover 2019.
Page 61 Carnage
The drawing is based on a picture I found on @unboxingbrosph
Page 62 Batgirl
The drawing is based on the magnificent cosplayer @realamandalynne
Page 63 Thanos
The drawing is based on a sculpture by Queen Studio
Page 64 Old men Spider-Man
Based on the concept art of Sergio Sykes
Page 65 Daredevil sonar
The drawing is based on a digital sculpture by artist Fabricio works
Page 66 Mr. Freeze
Based on a statue from @sideshow
Page 67 Storm
Sketch based on a digital sculpture by the amazing artist @francocarlesimo
Page 68 Ironfist variant
Page 69 The Wolverine close up
Drawing based on a digital sculpture by artist Franco Carlesimo
Page 70 The Bat in the Shadows
Page 71 General Kenobi
The drawing is based on the digital art by Battlefront. pictures
Page 72 A vs X
Characters are modeled on various busts and statues from @ironstudios @nmk_studios @xmstudios and others.
Page 73 Batgirl in the Shadows
Based on the amazing cosplayer @epc_cosplay
Page 74 Vader
Based on a digital drawing by @maciejdrabik_art
Page 75 Blade Runner
Sketches inspired by Ana De Armas in Blade Runner 2049
Page 76 Chirrut Îmwe, Rogue One
Page 77 Gabriel Dagenais
Page 78 Thomas Alexandre Dagenais
Page 79 Mikaël Dagenais
Page 80 Debby Lyons
Page 81 Acknowledgments
Page 82 Legal Mentions

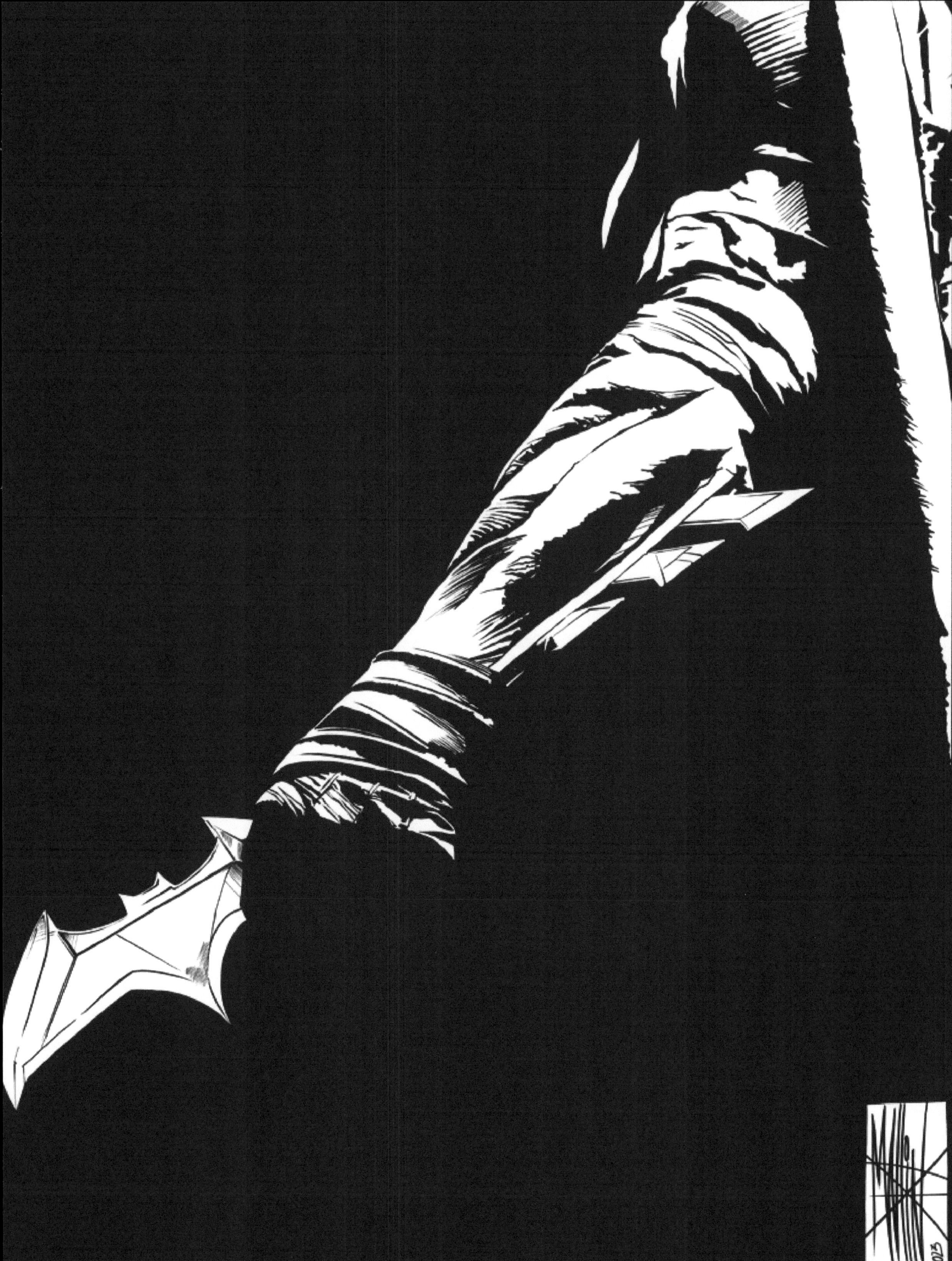

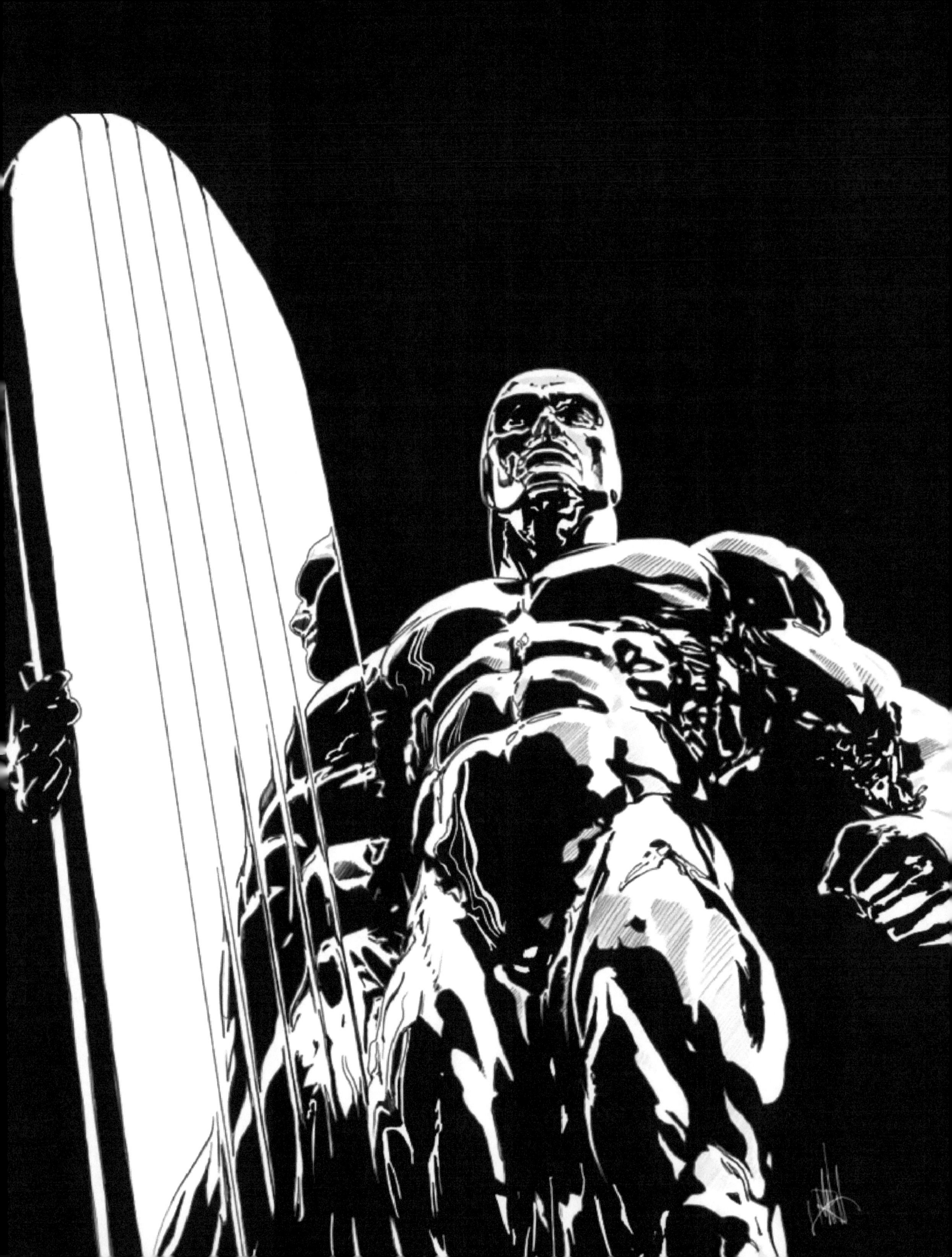

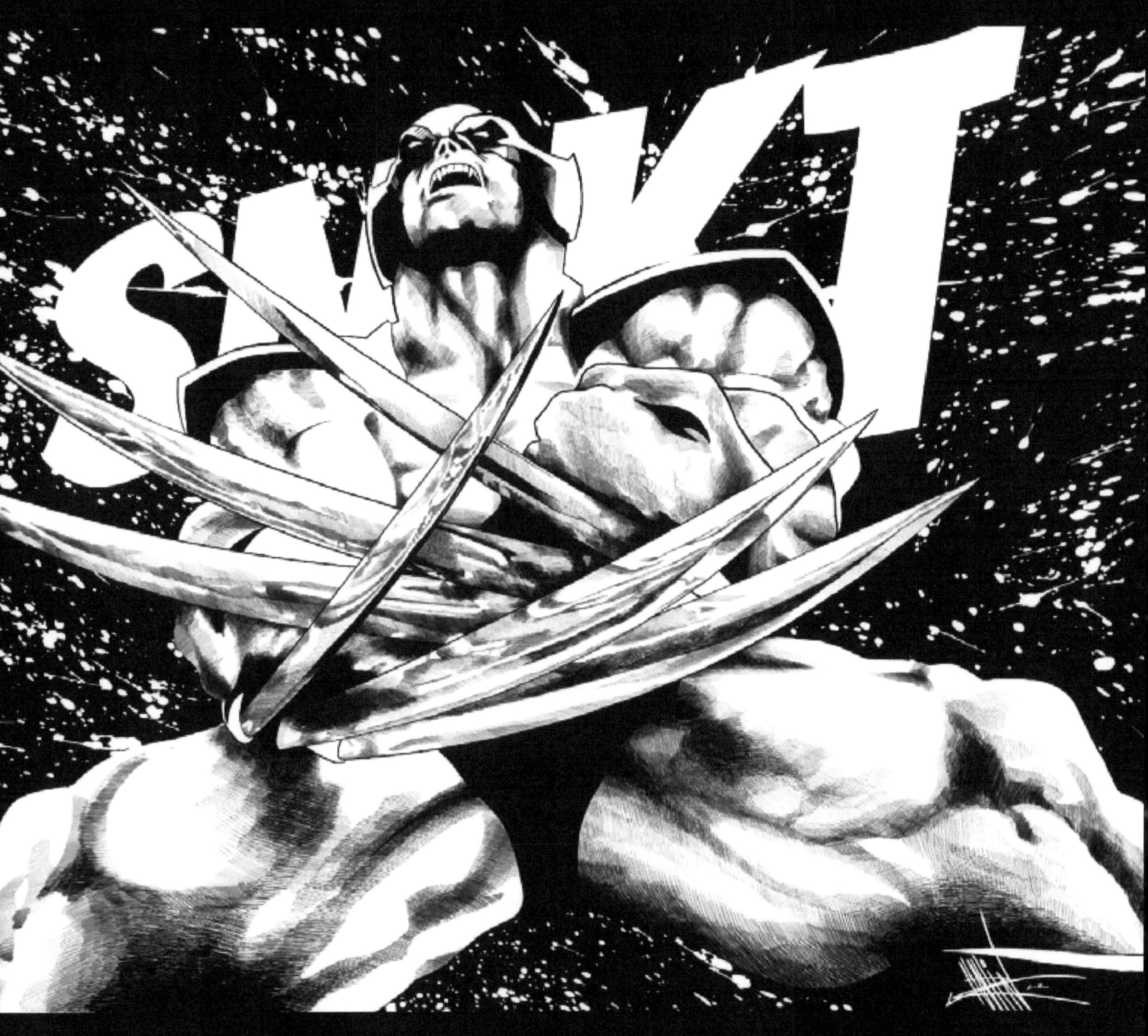

SNIKT

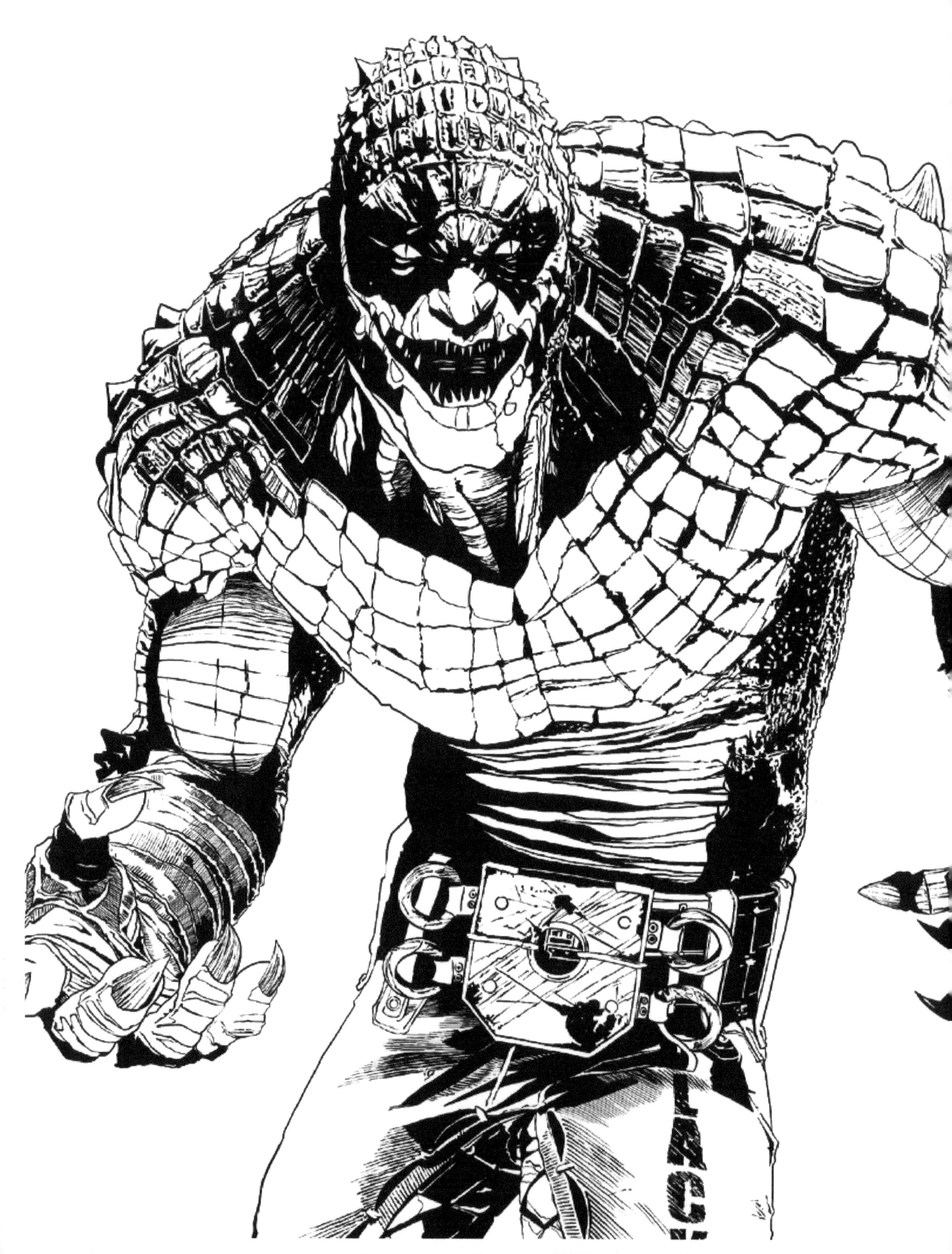

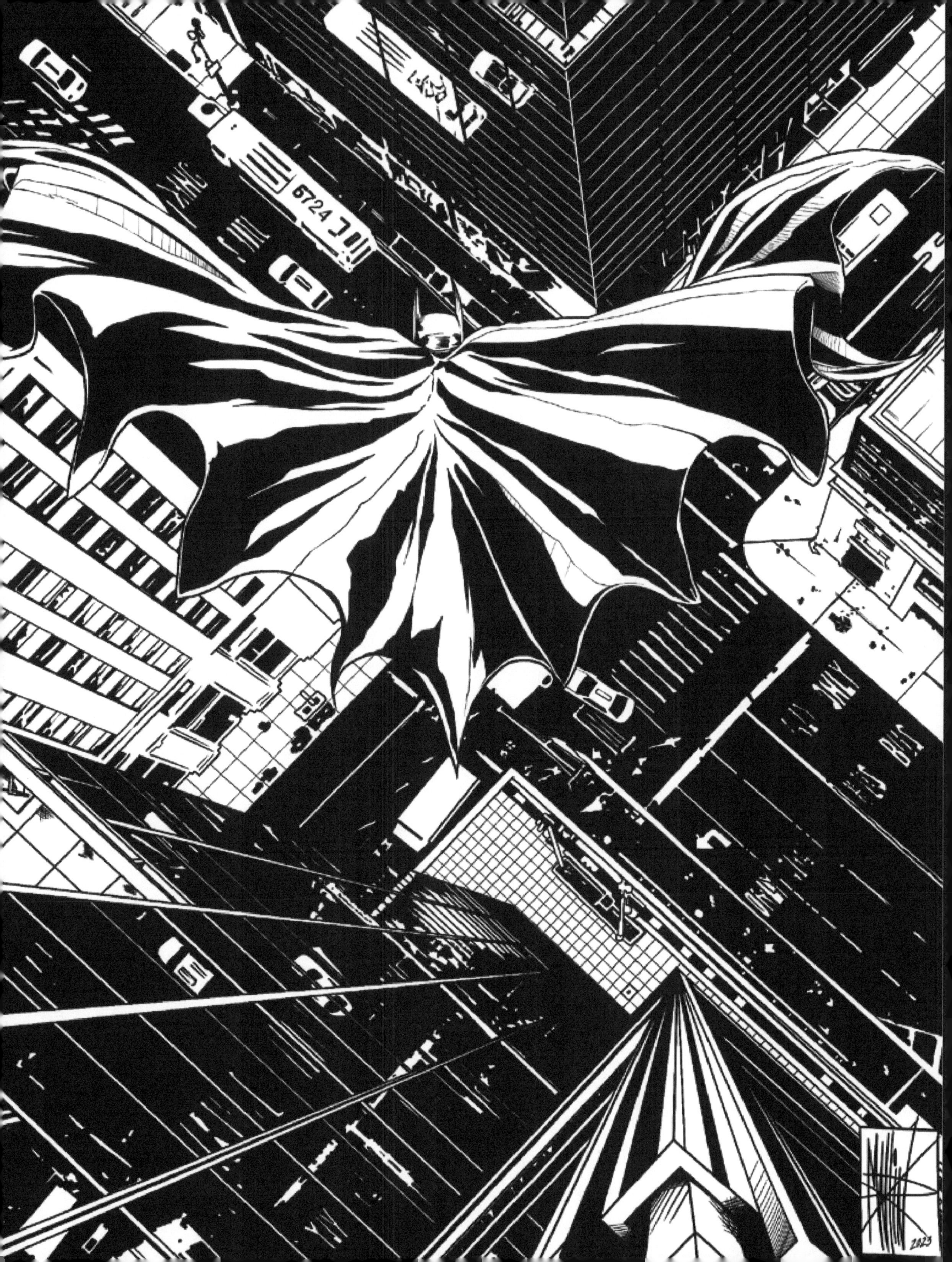
6724

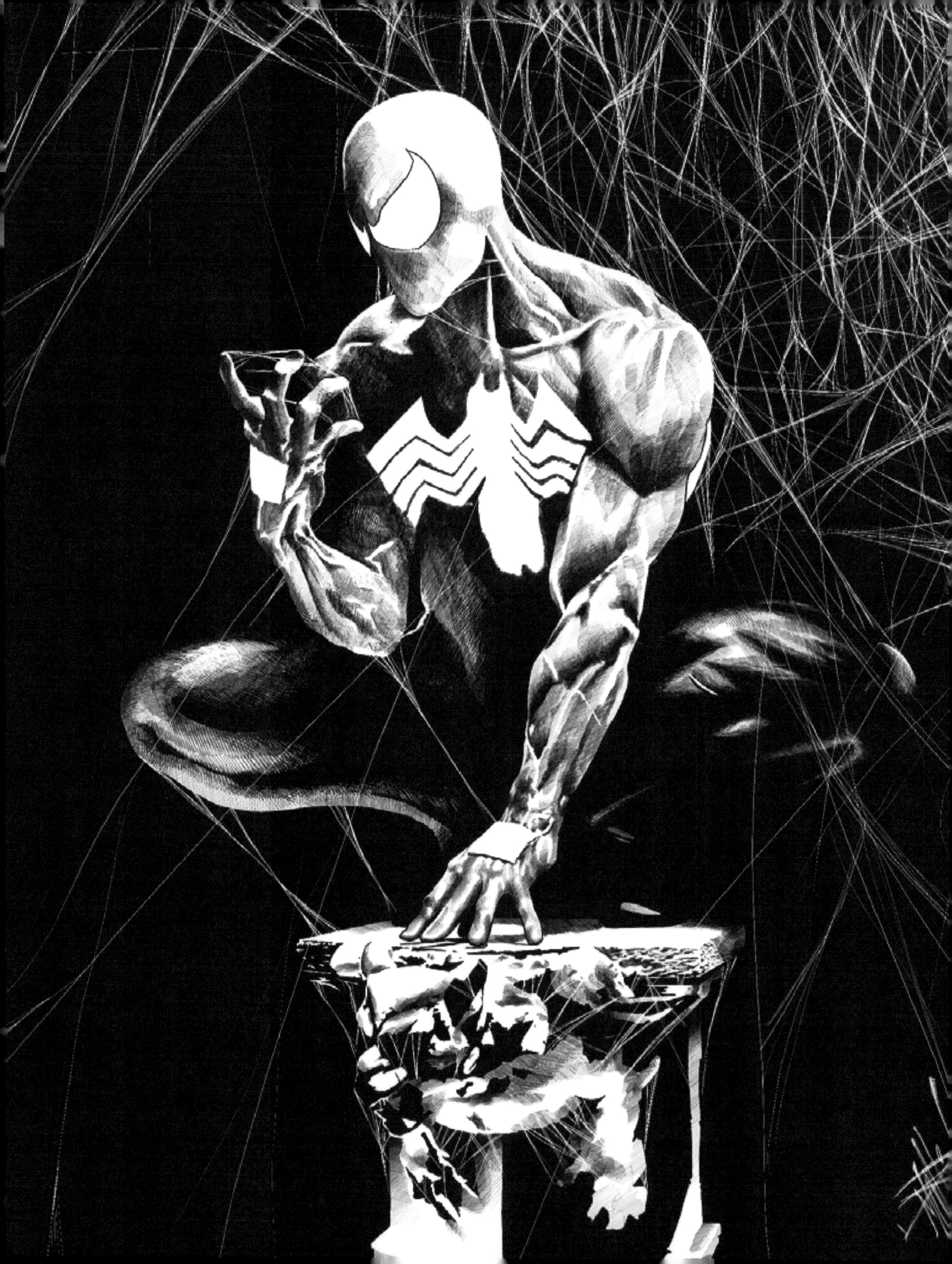

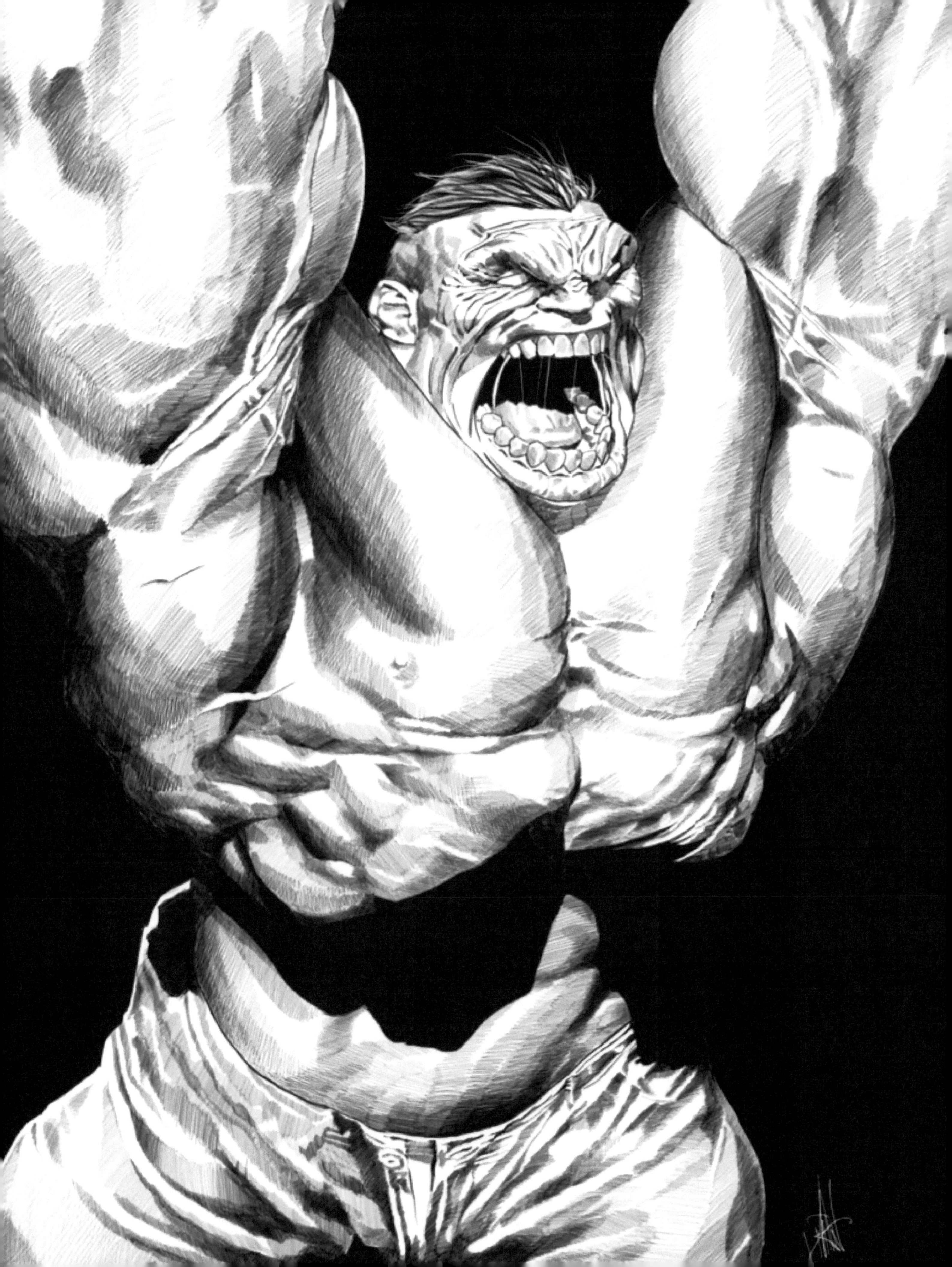

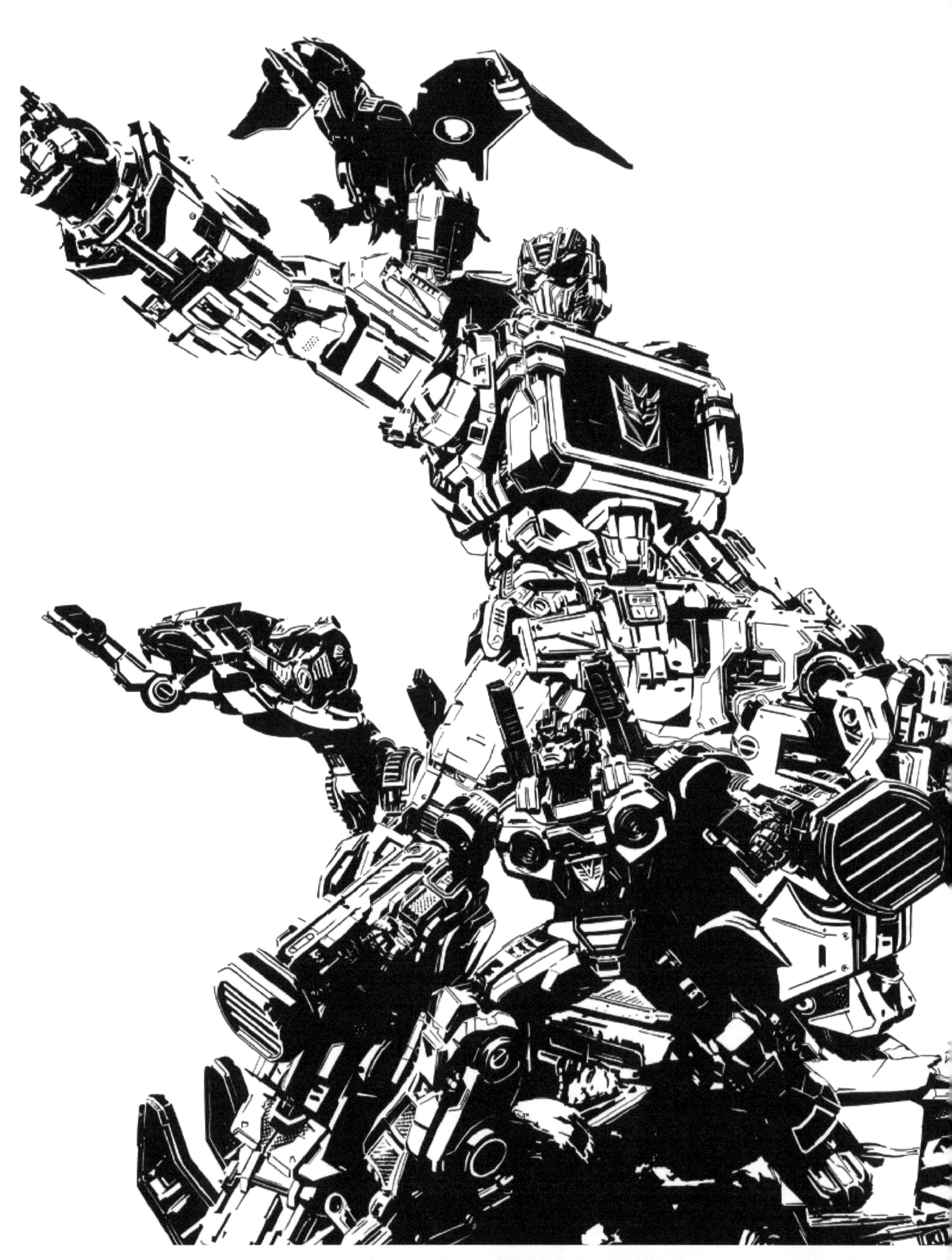

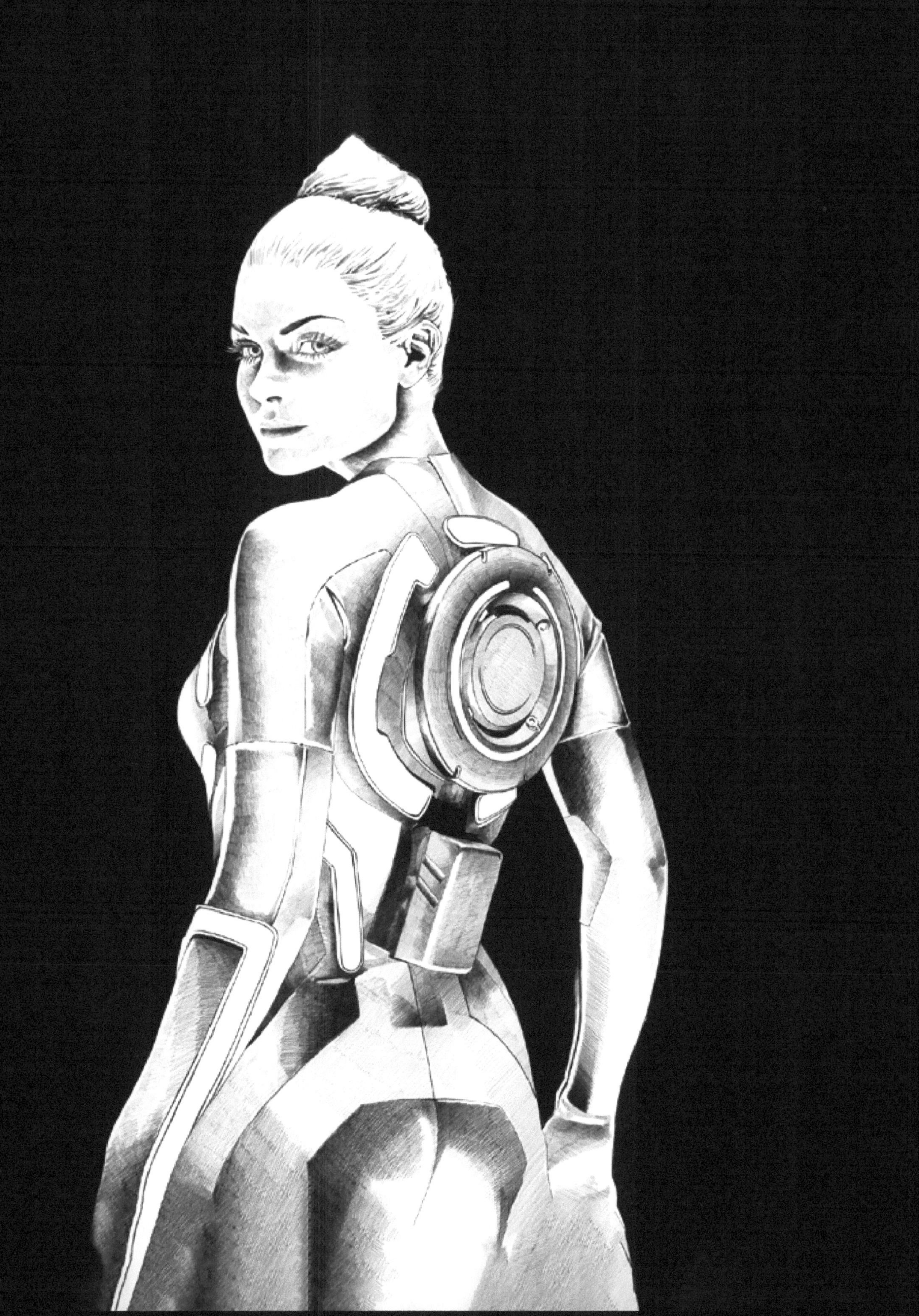

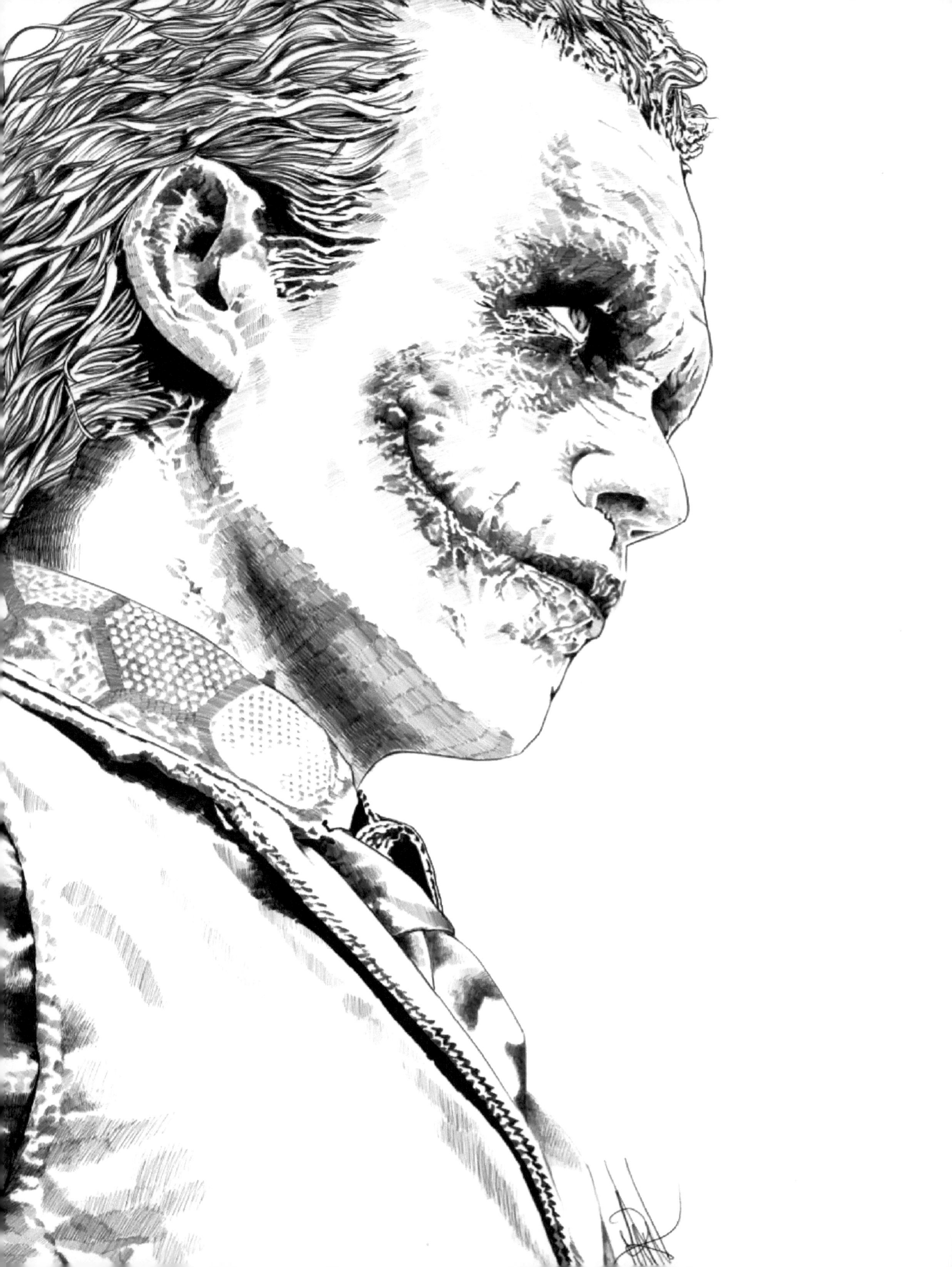

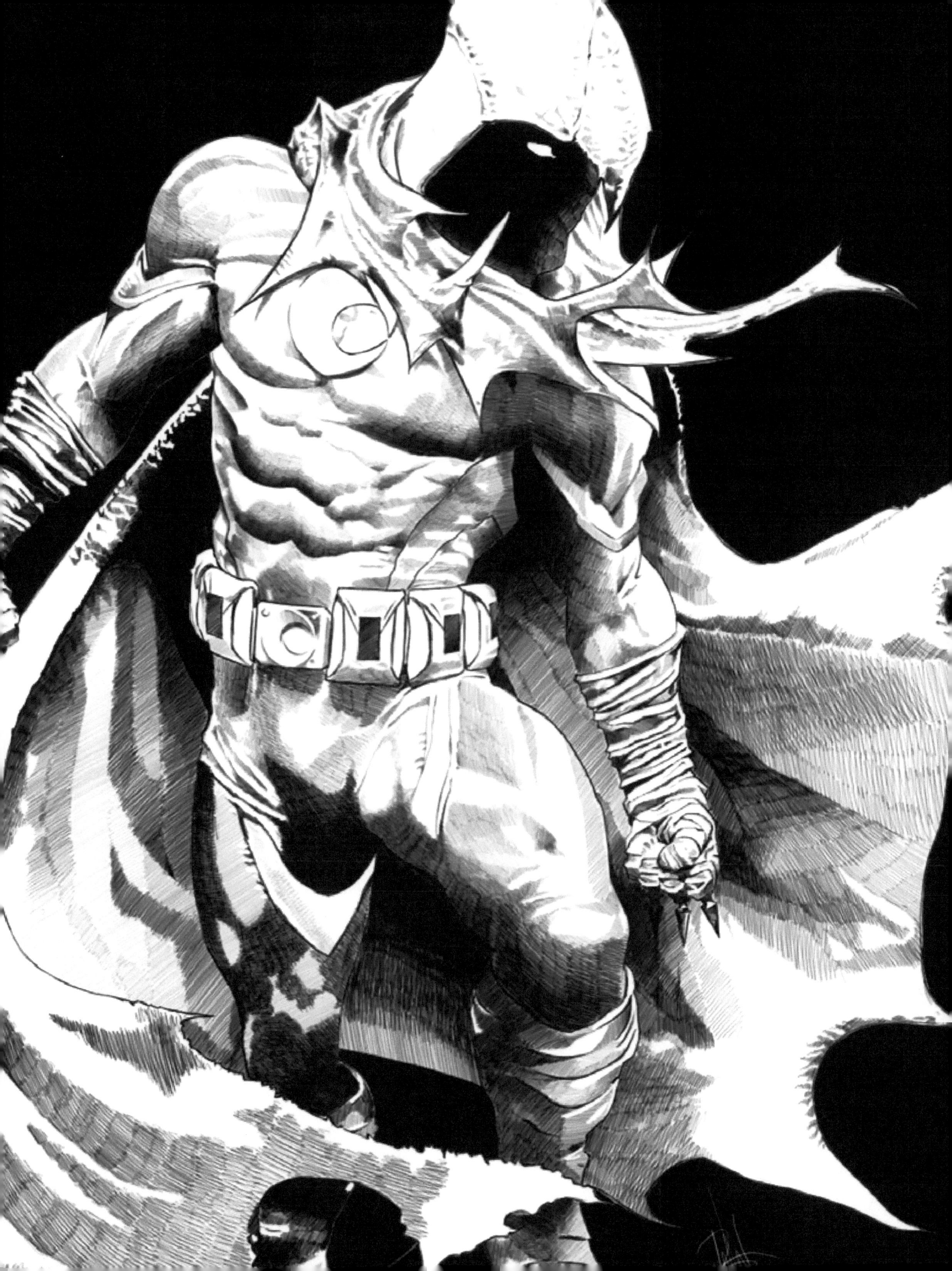

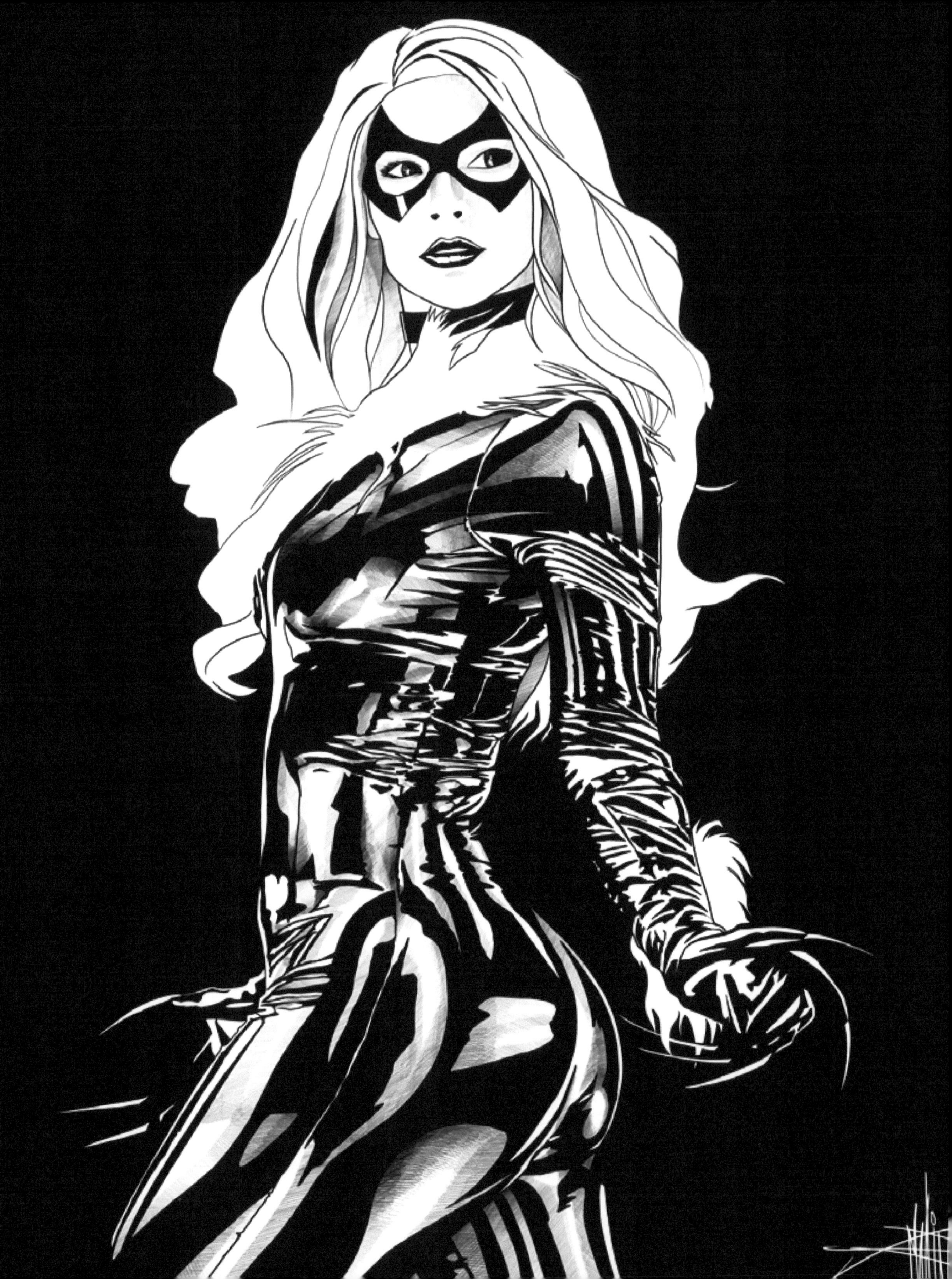

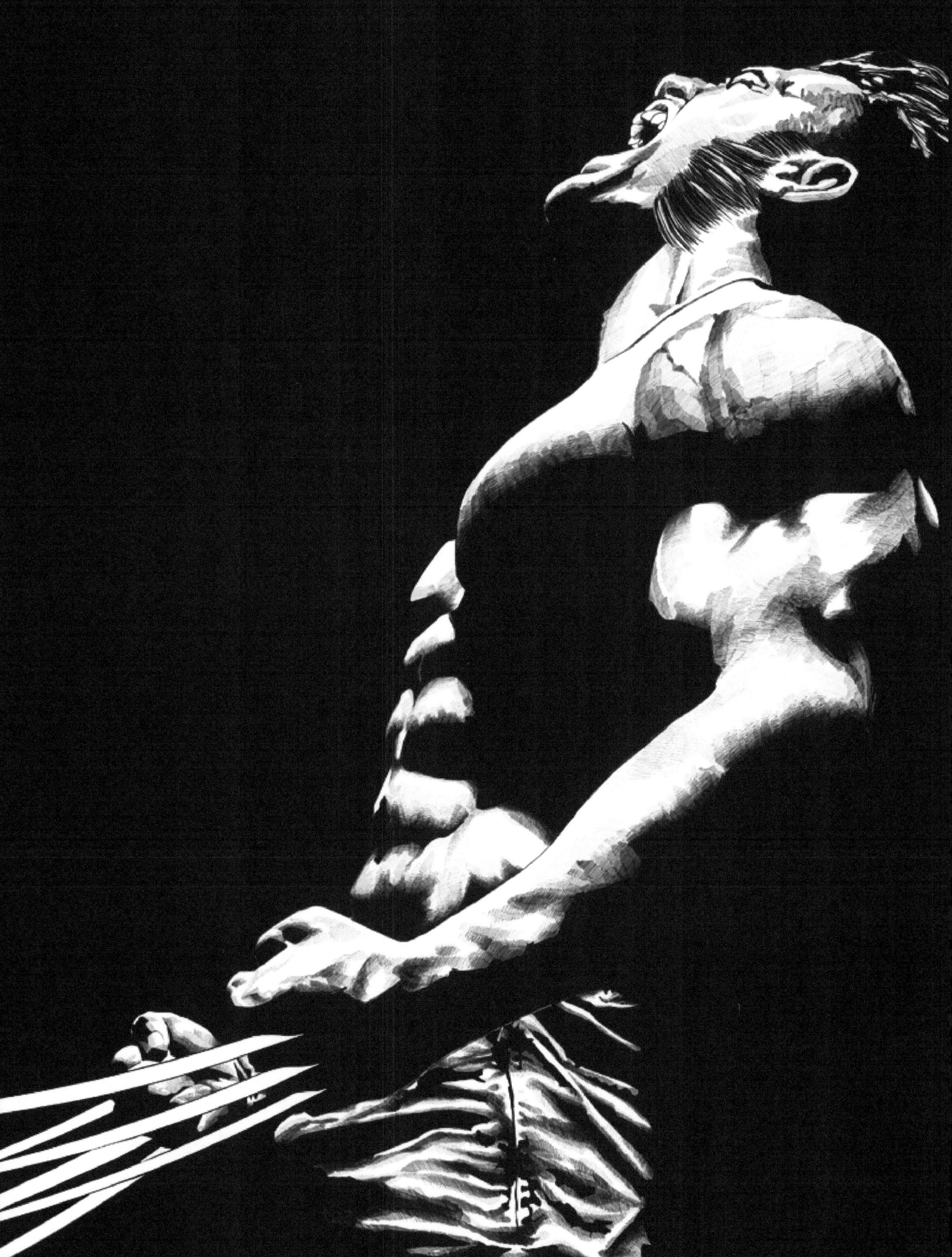

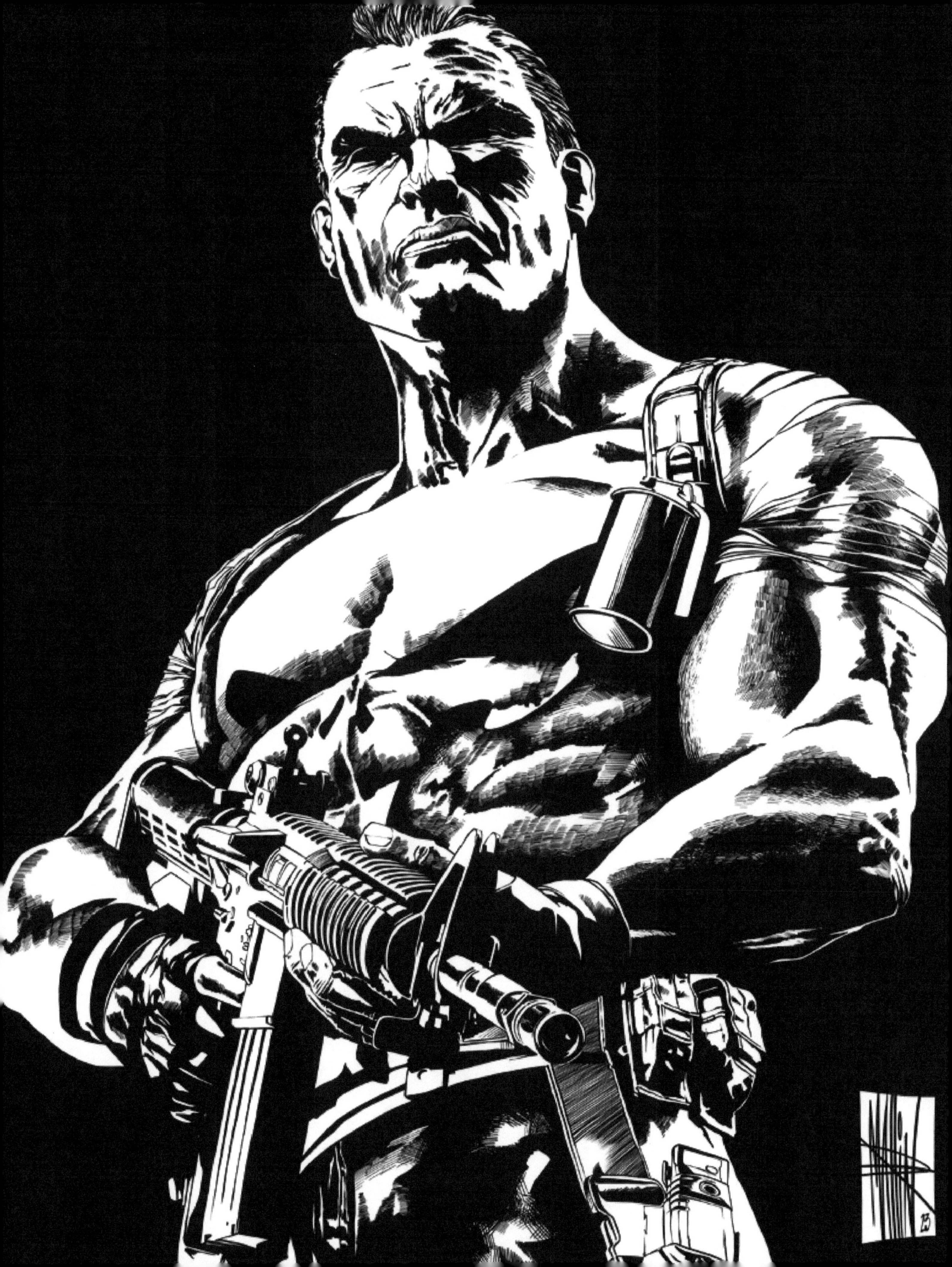

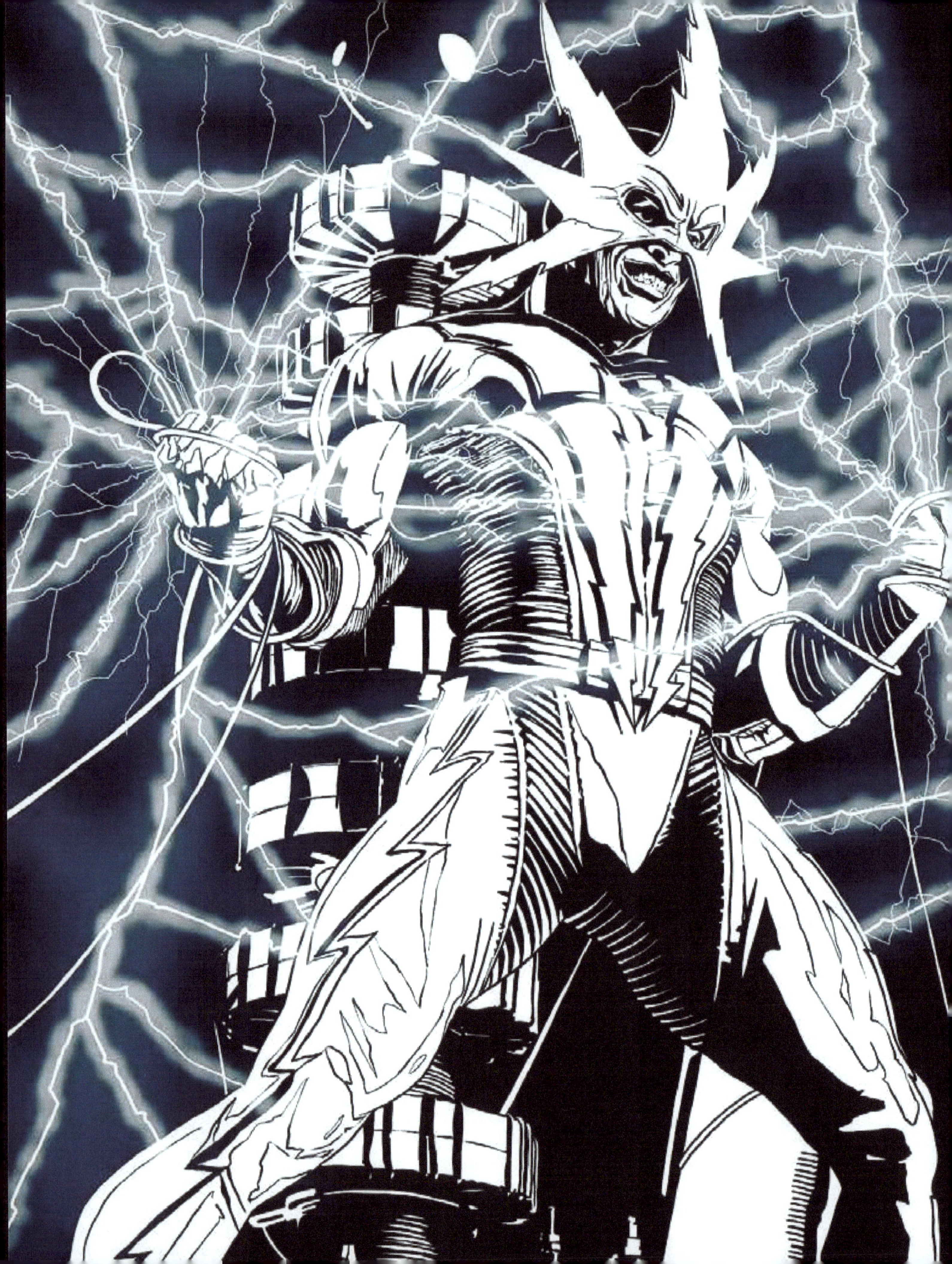

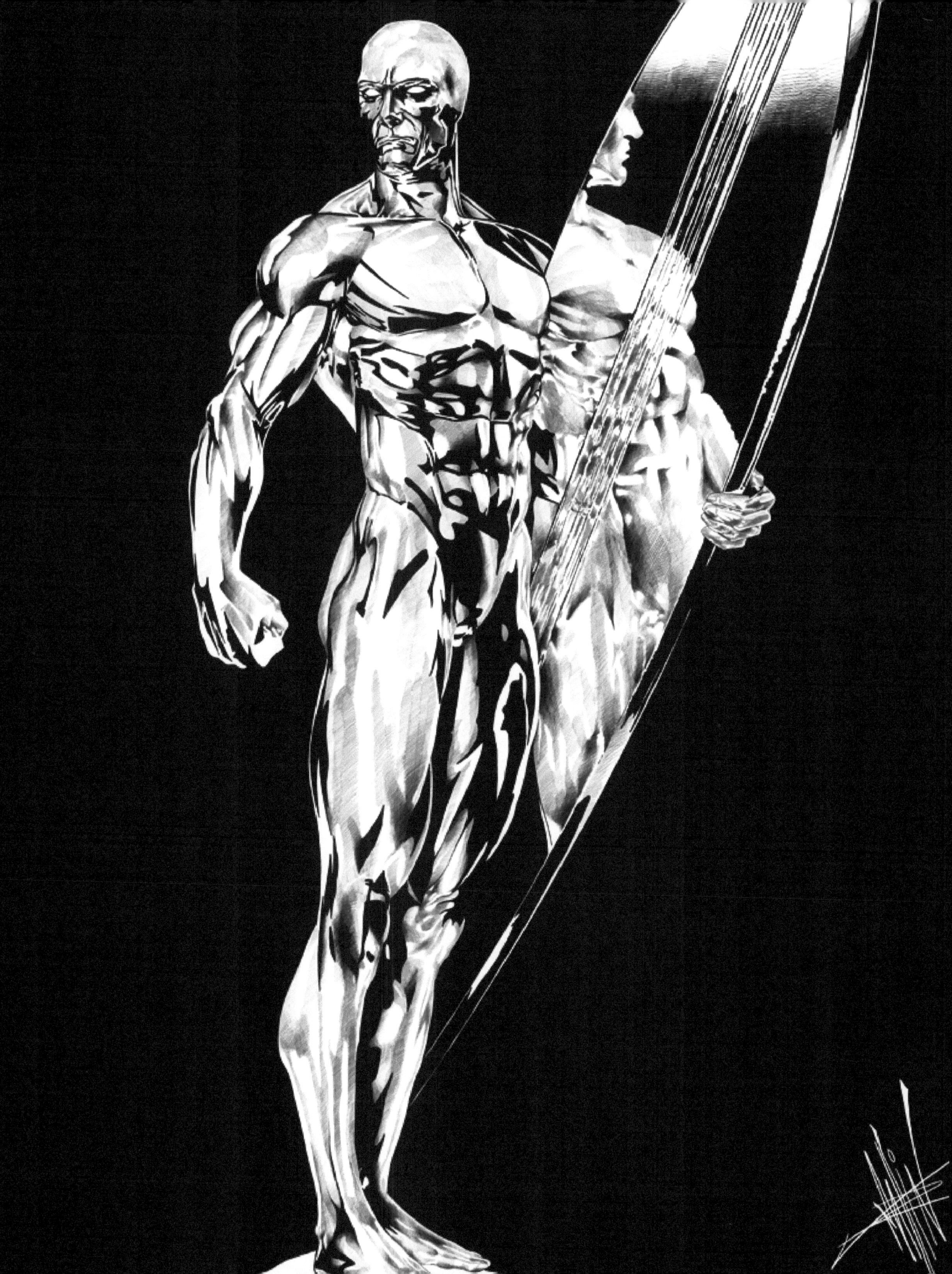

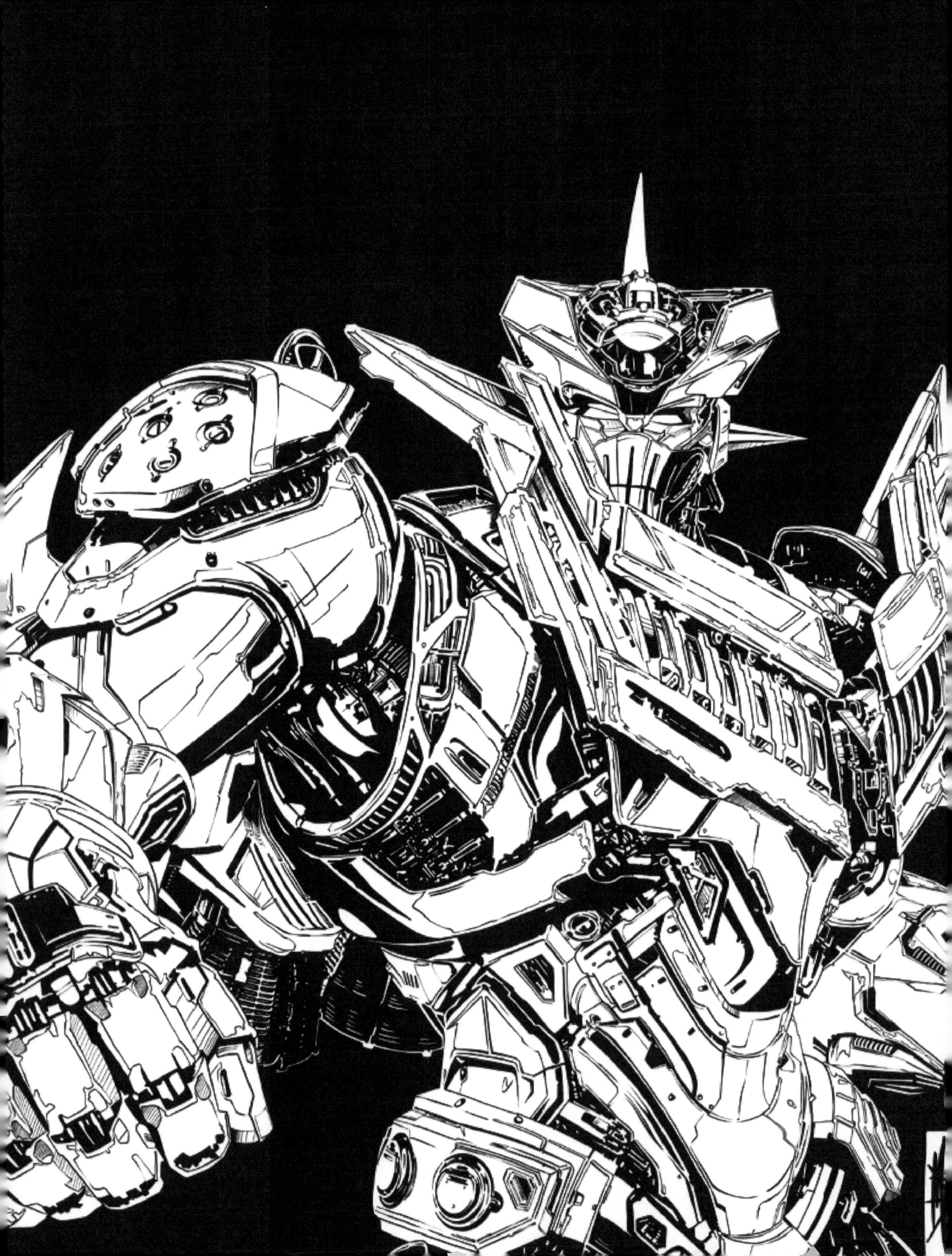

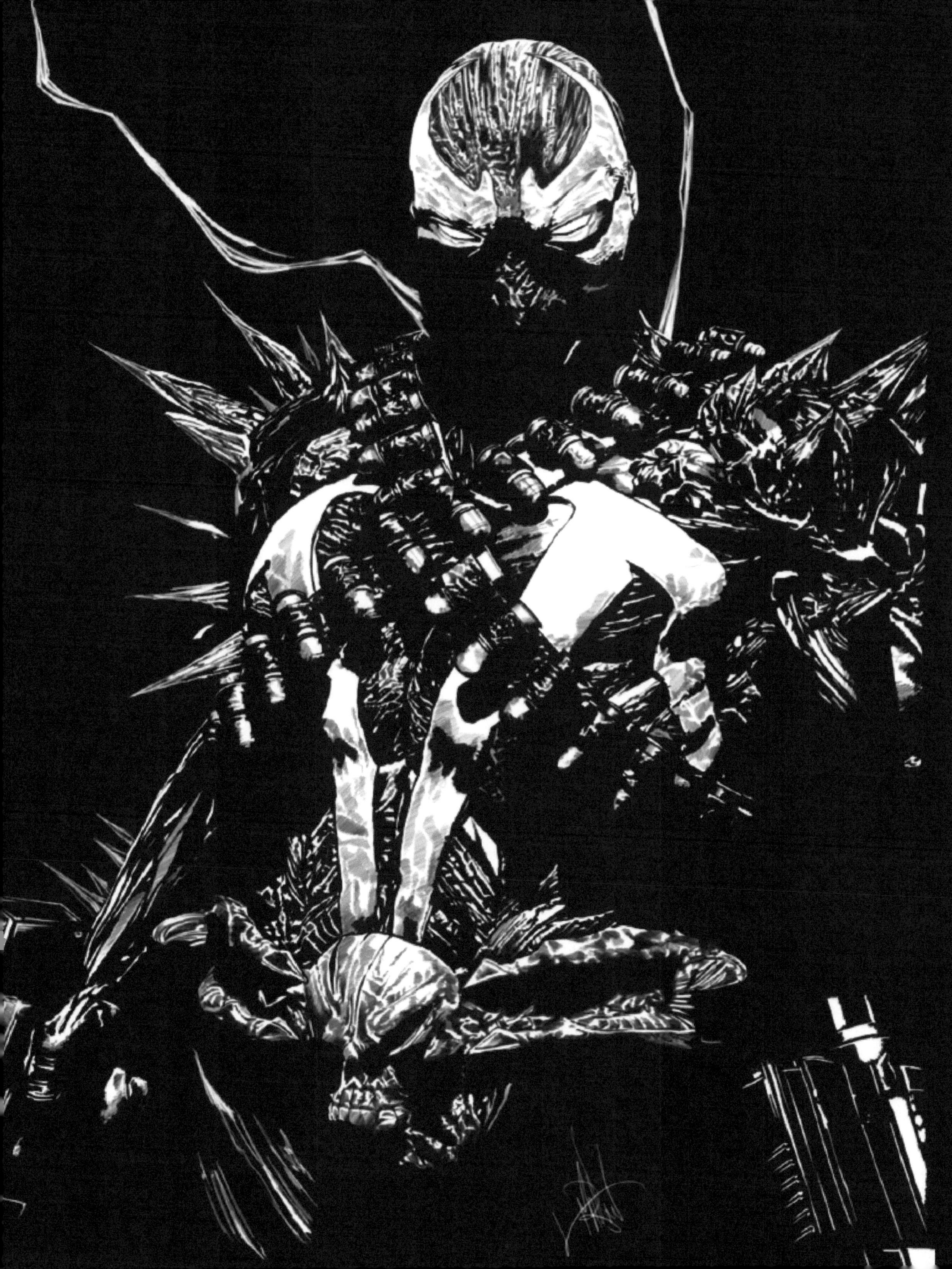

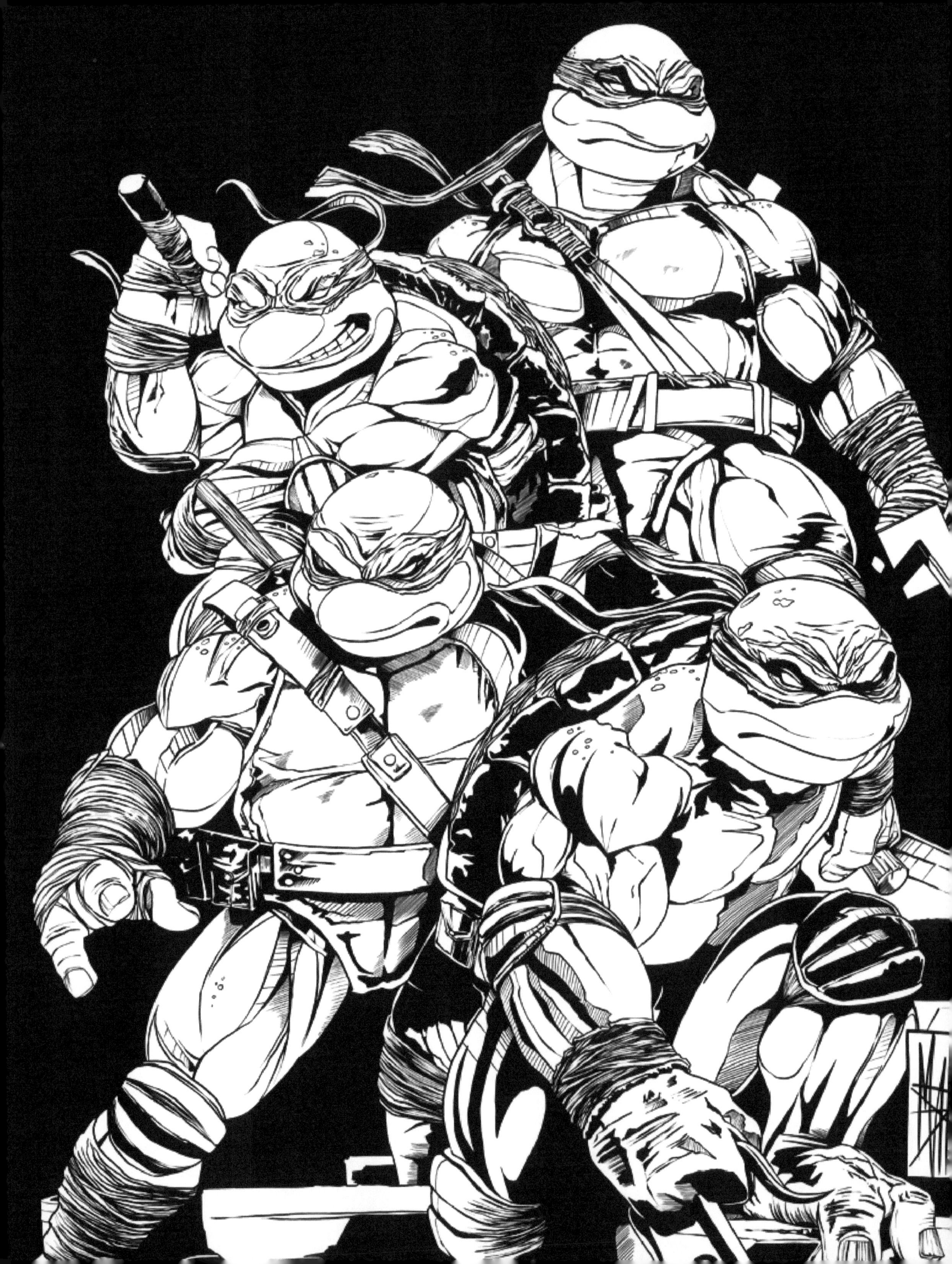

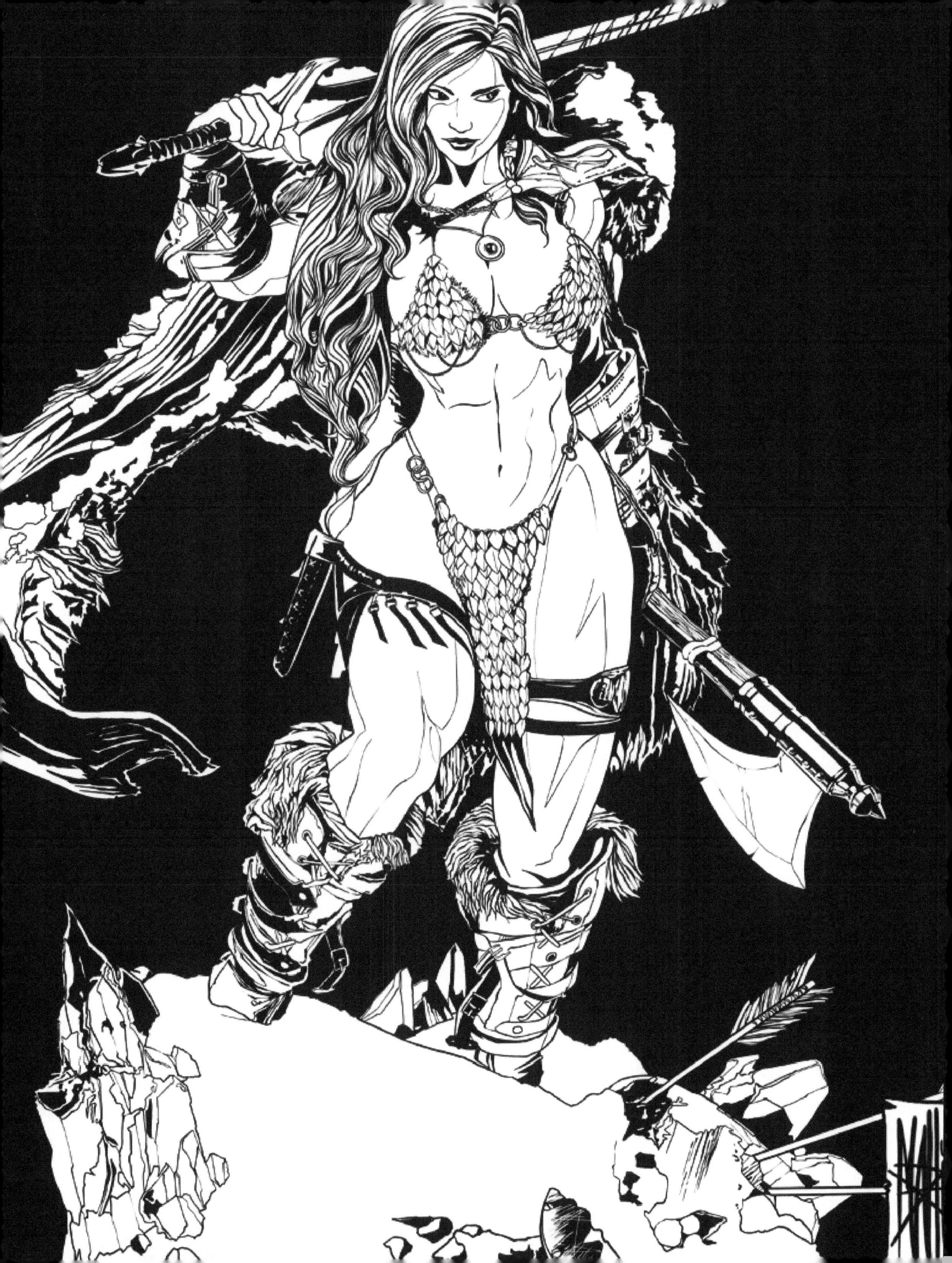

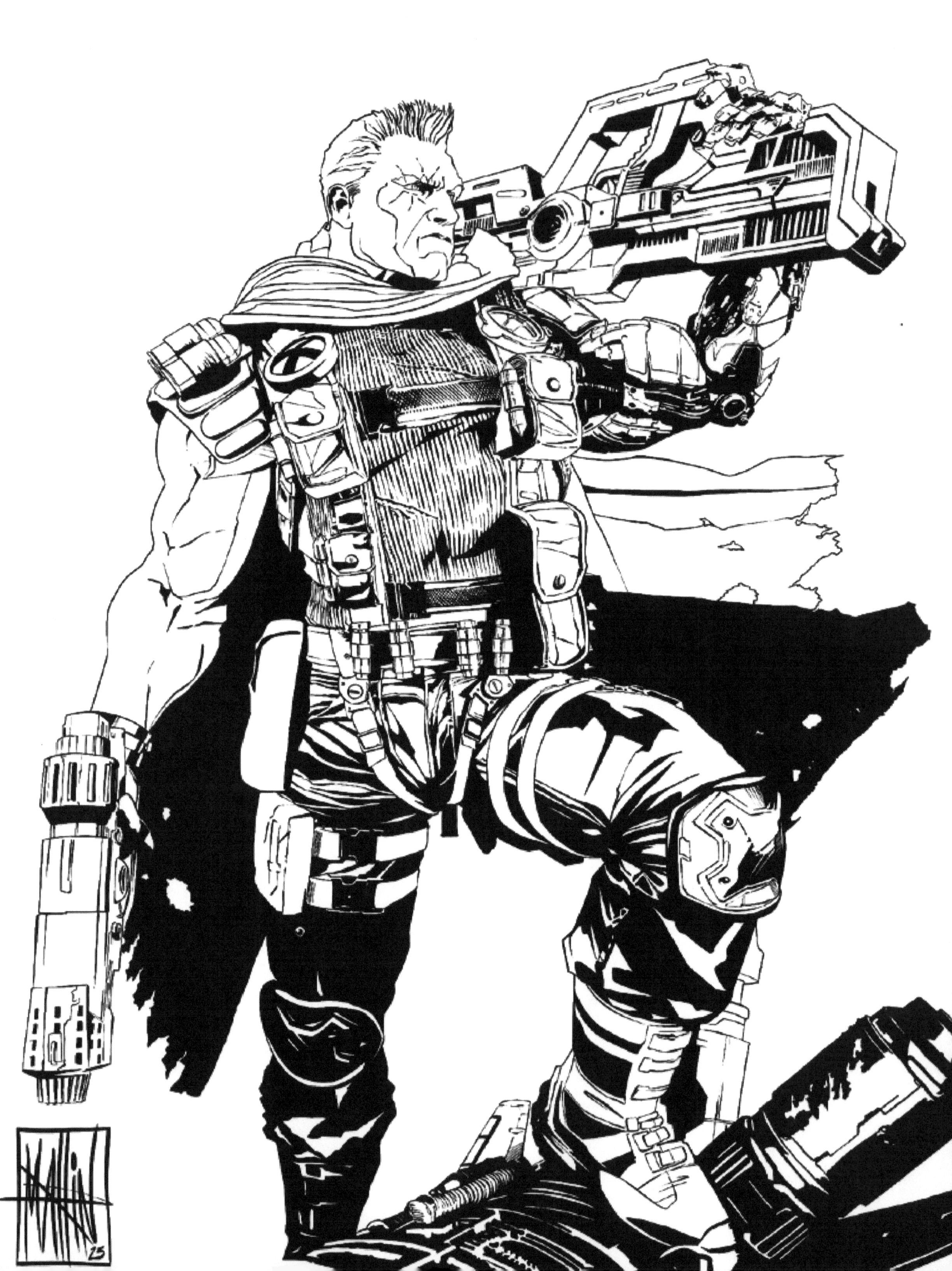

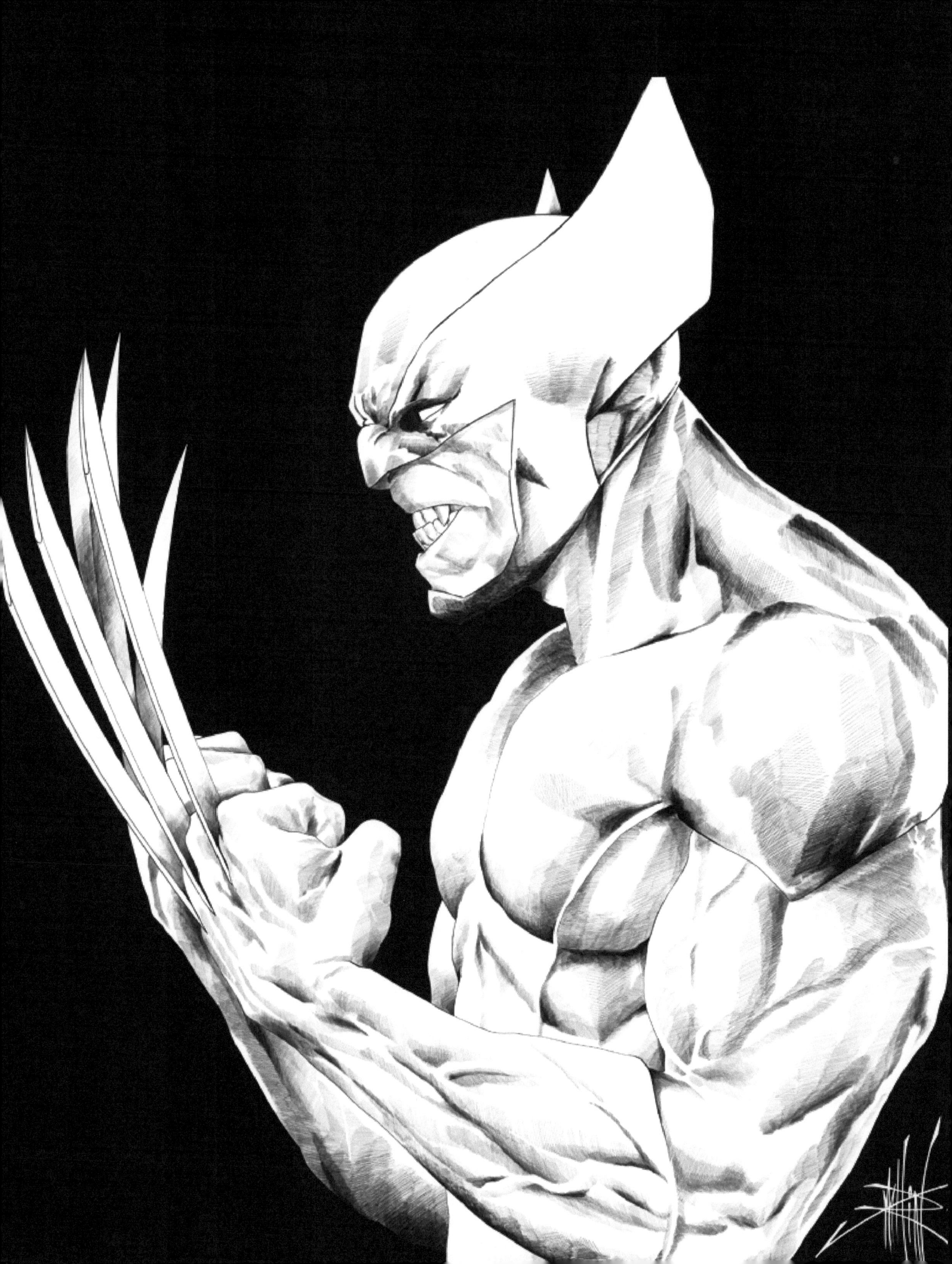

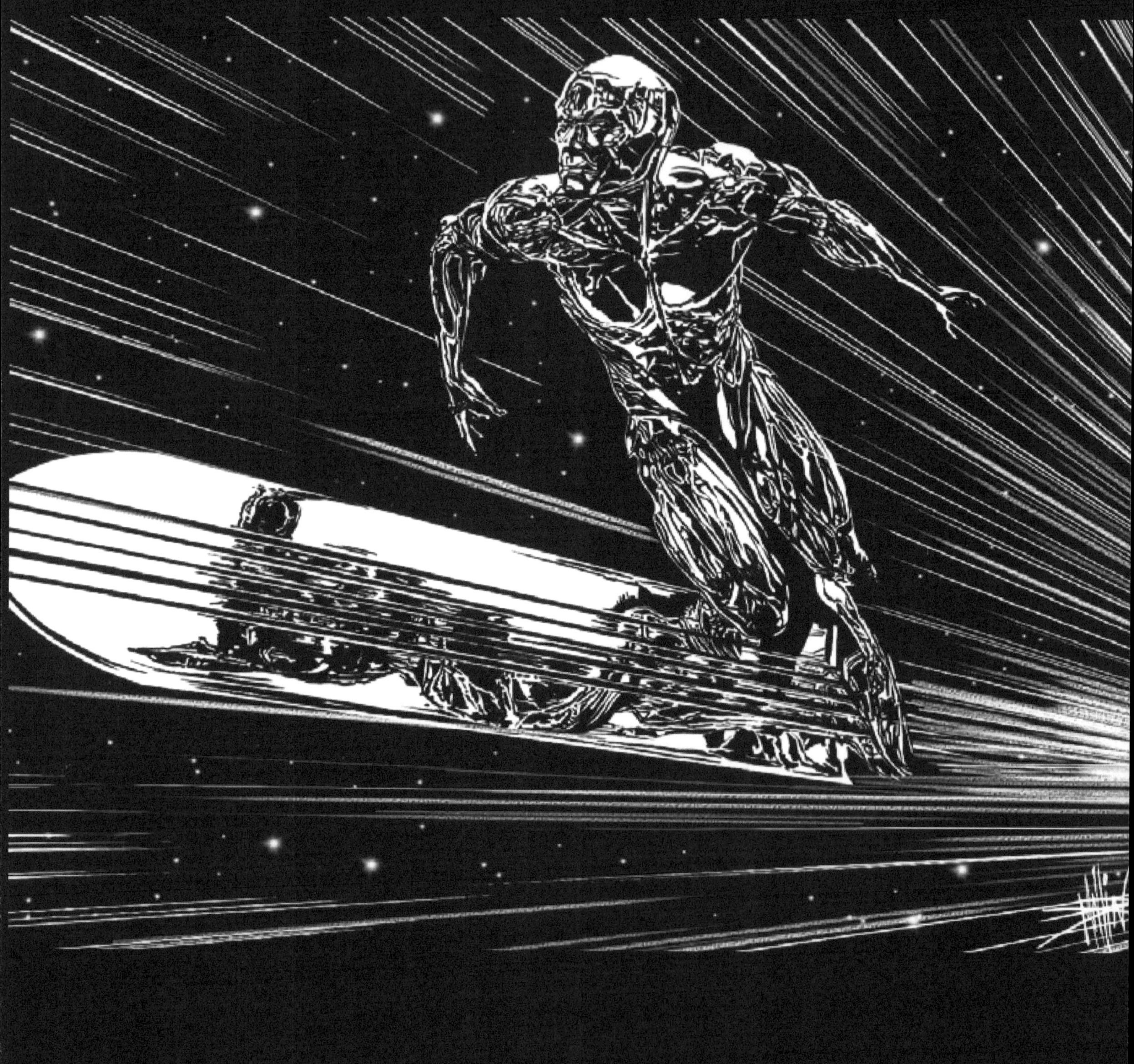

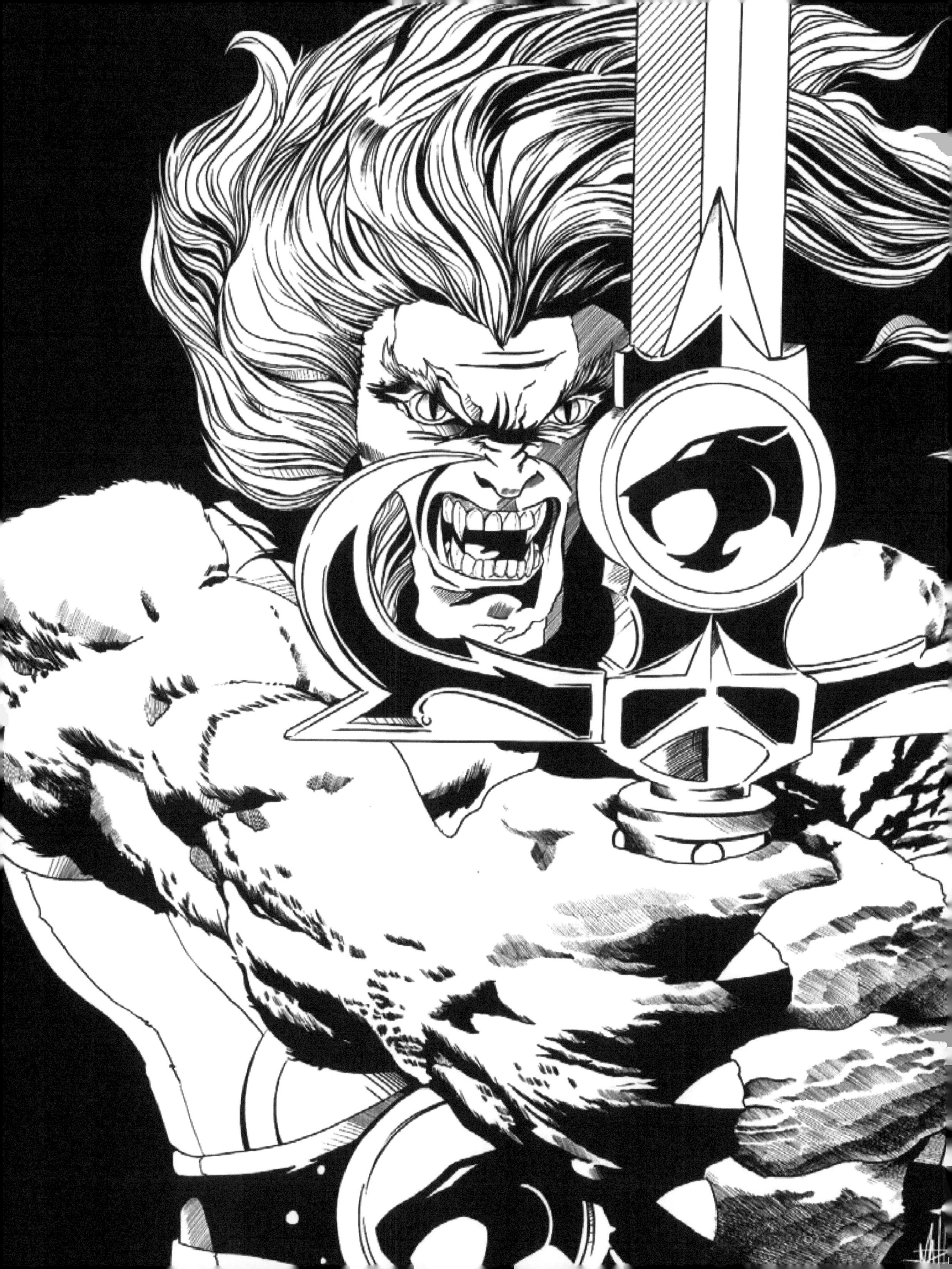

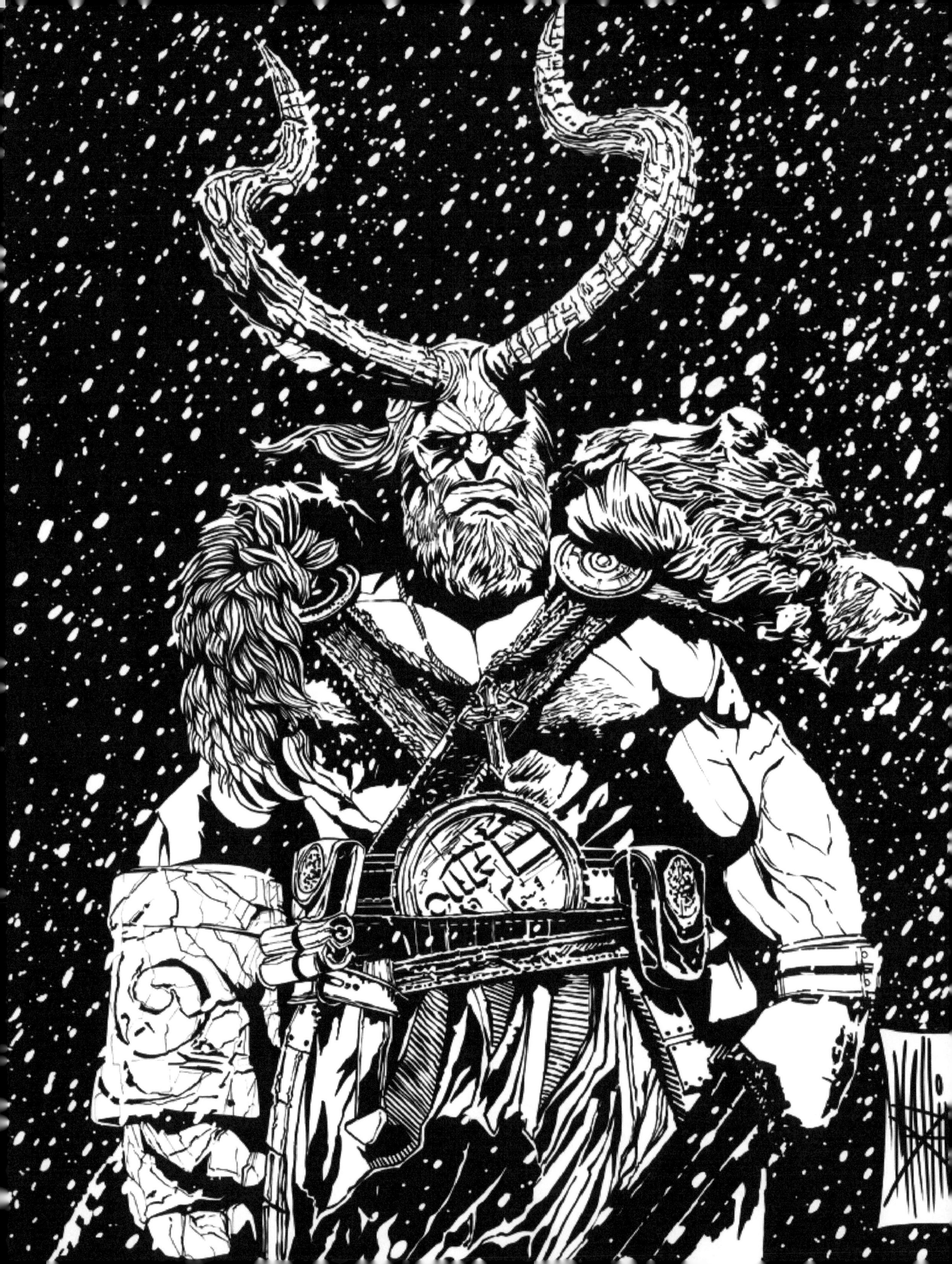

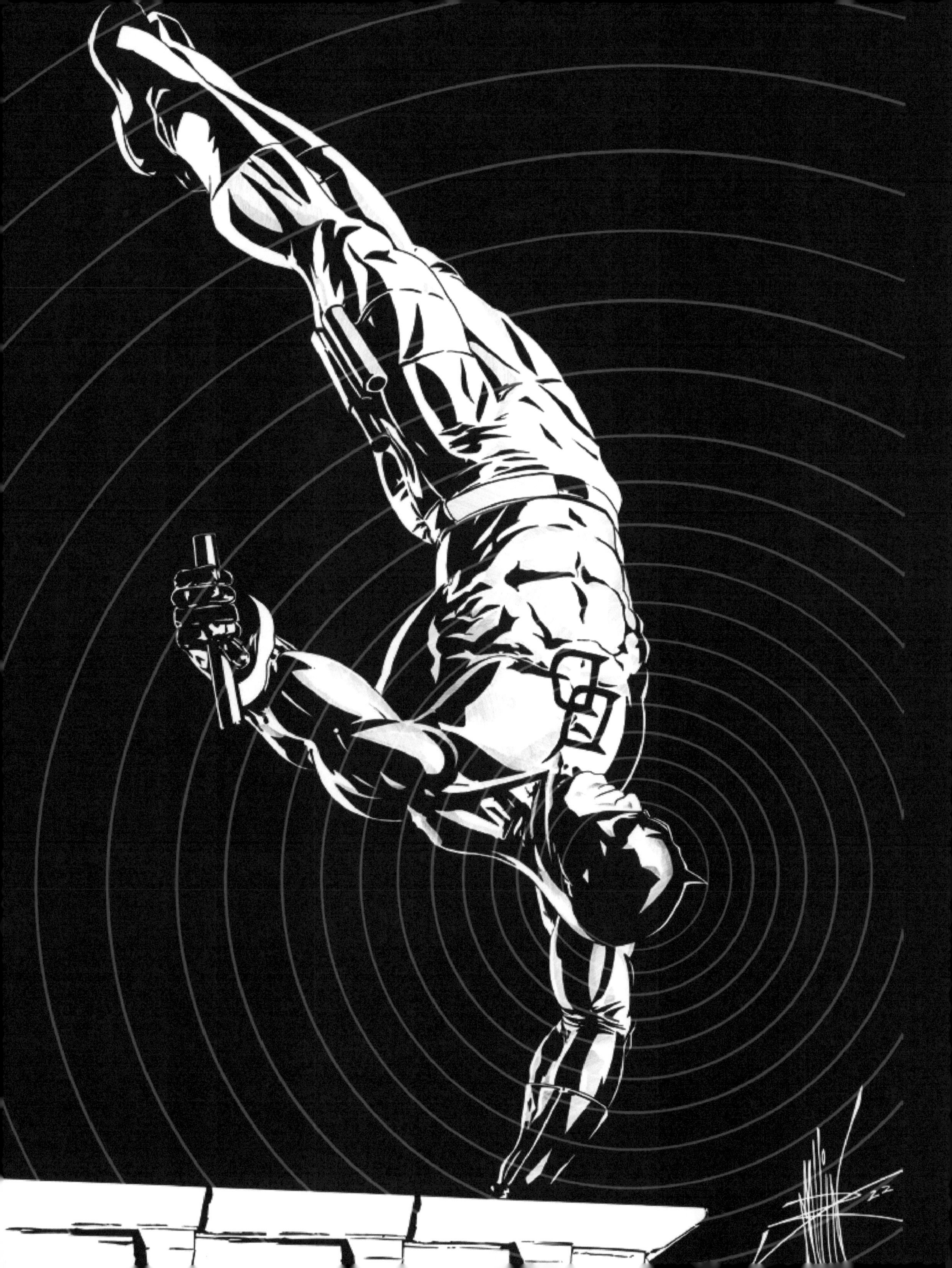

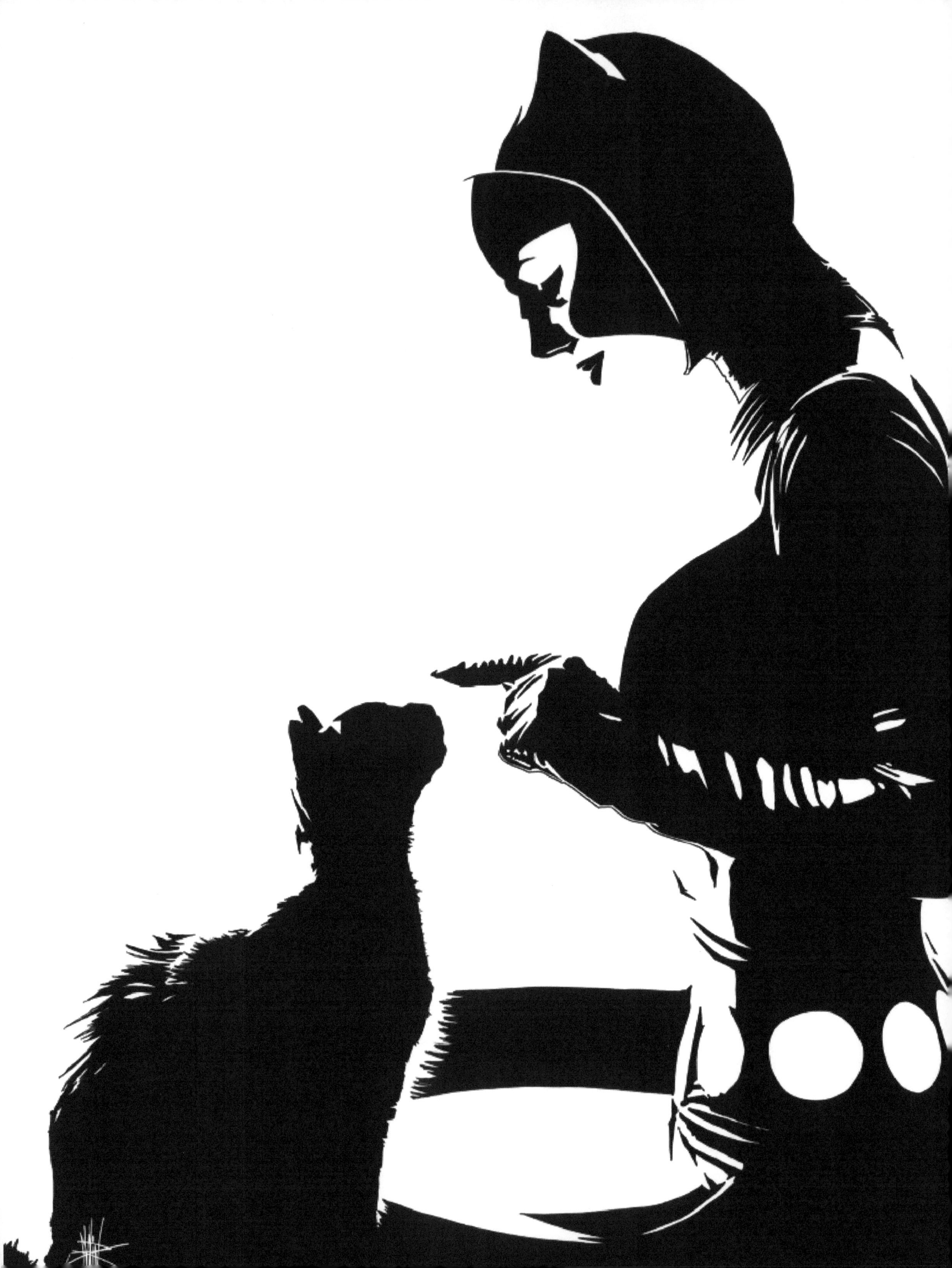

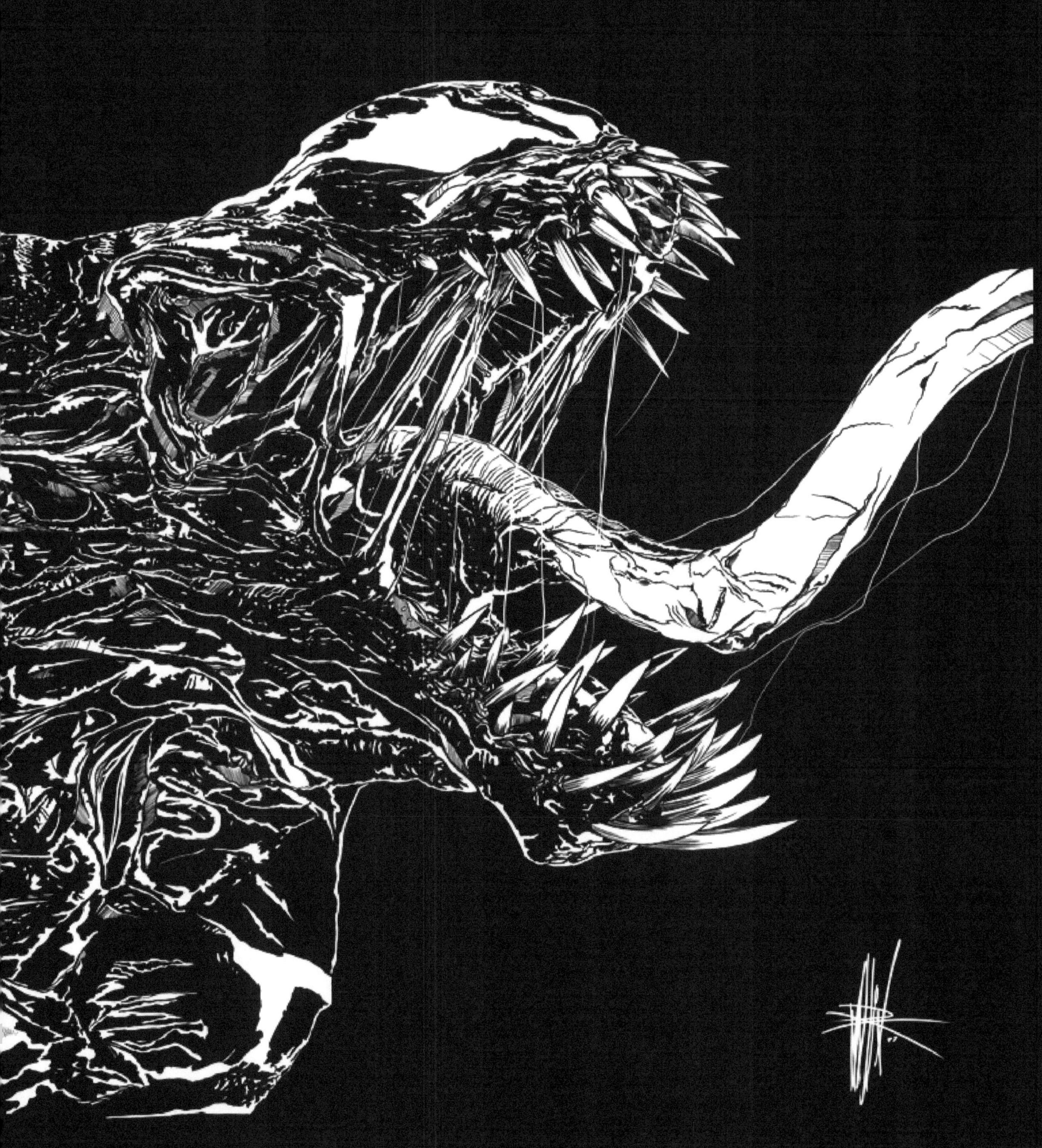

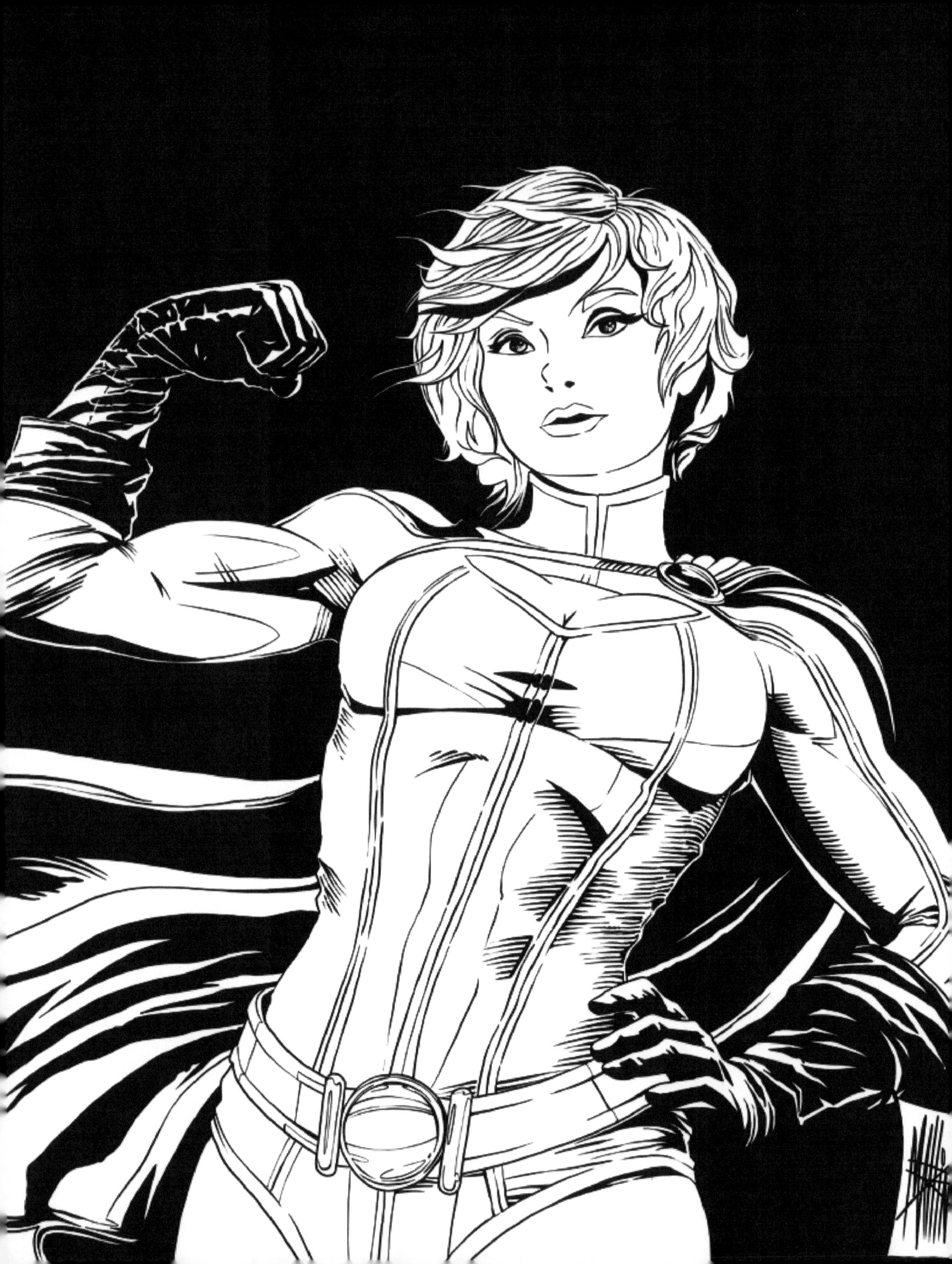

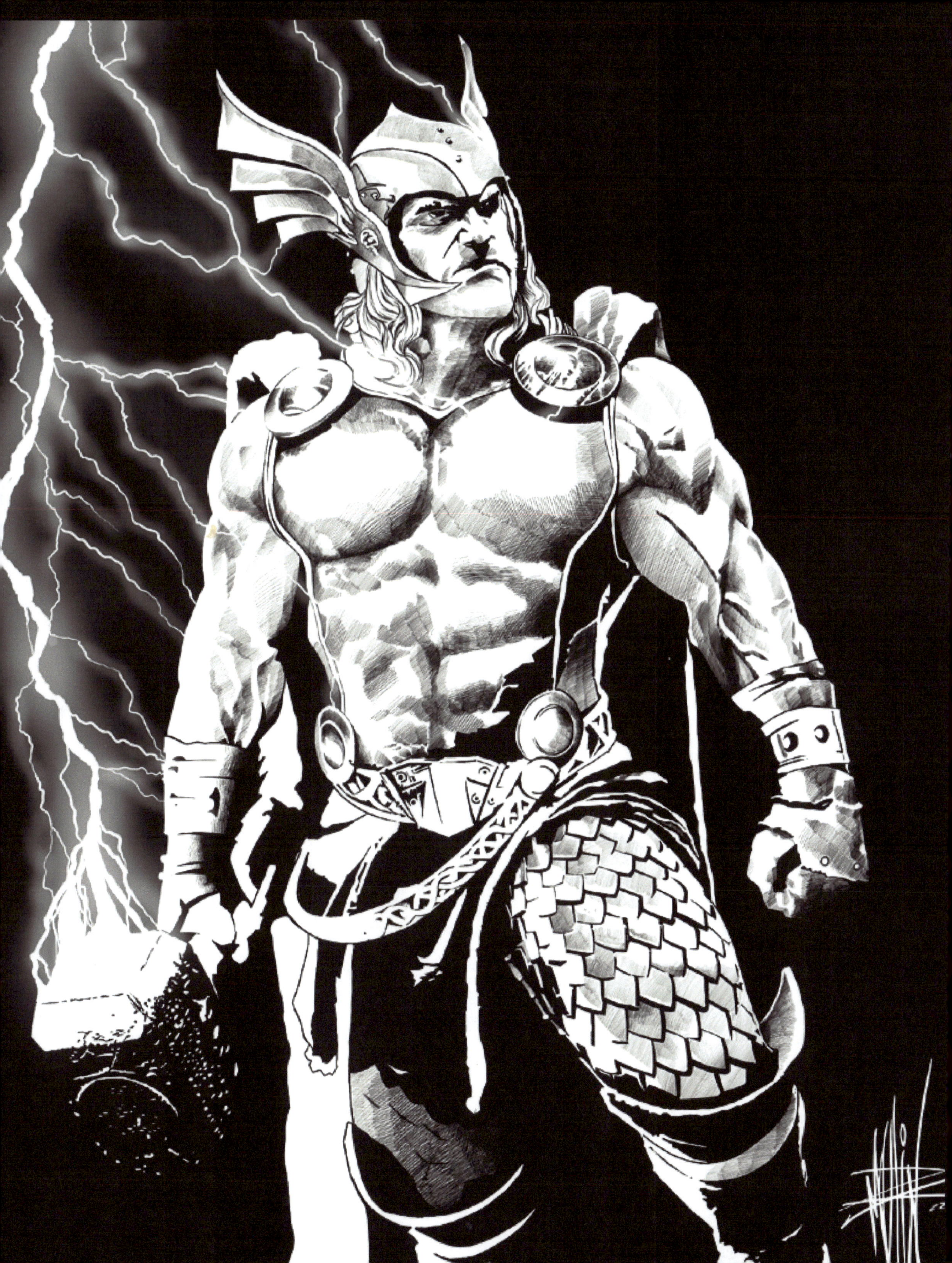

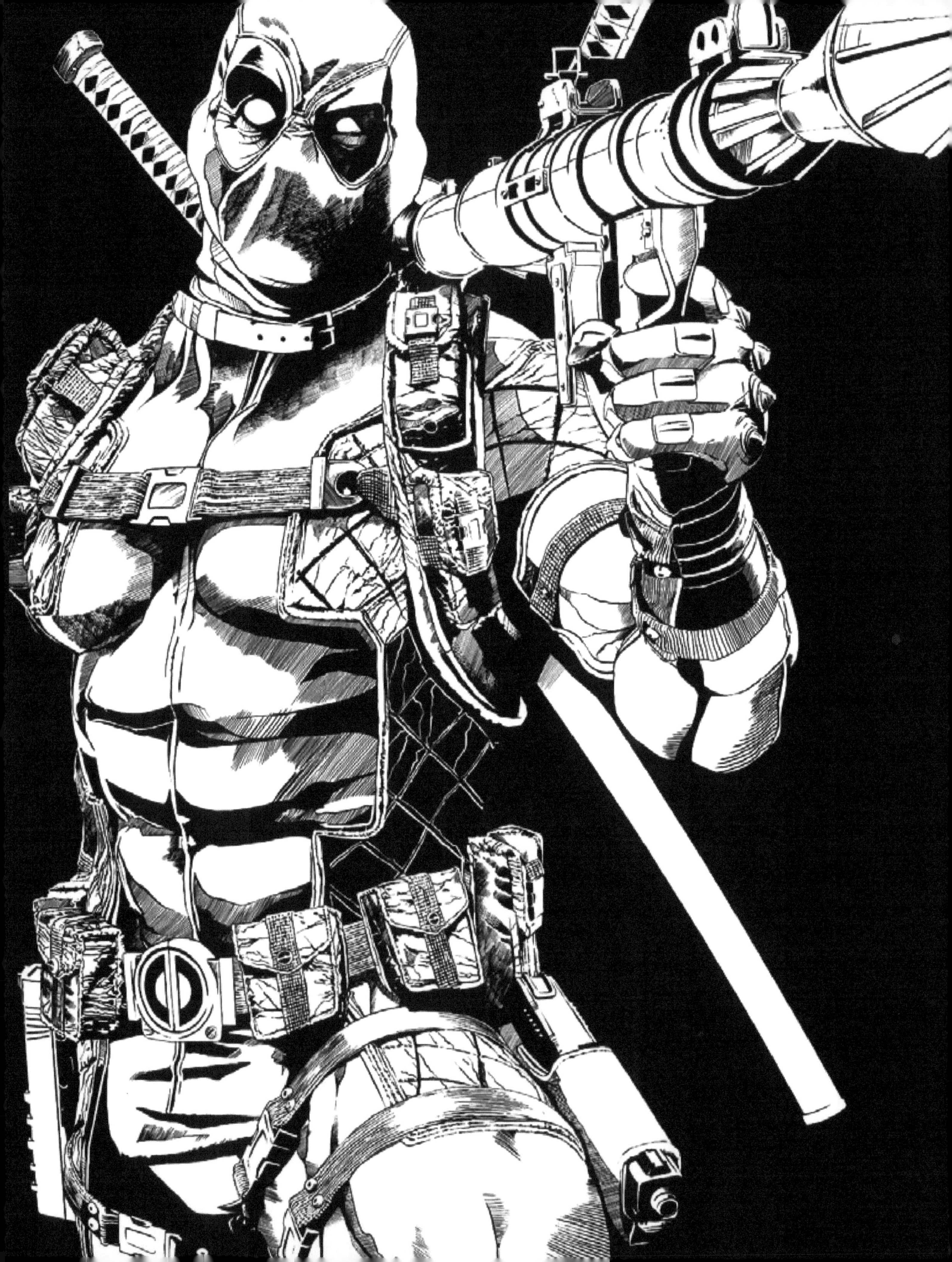

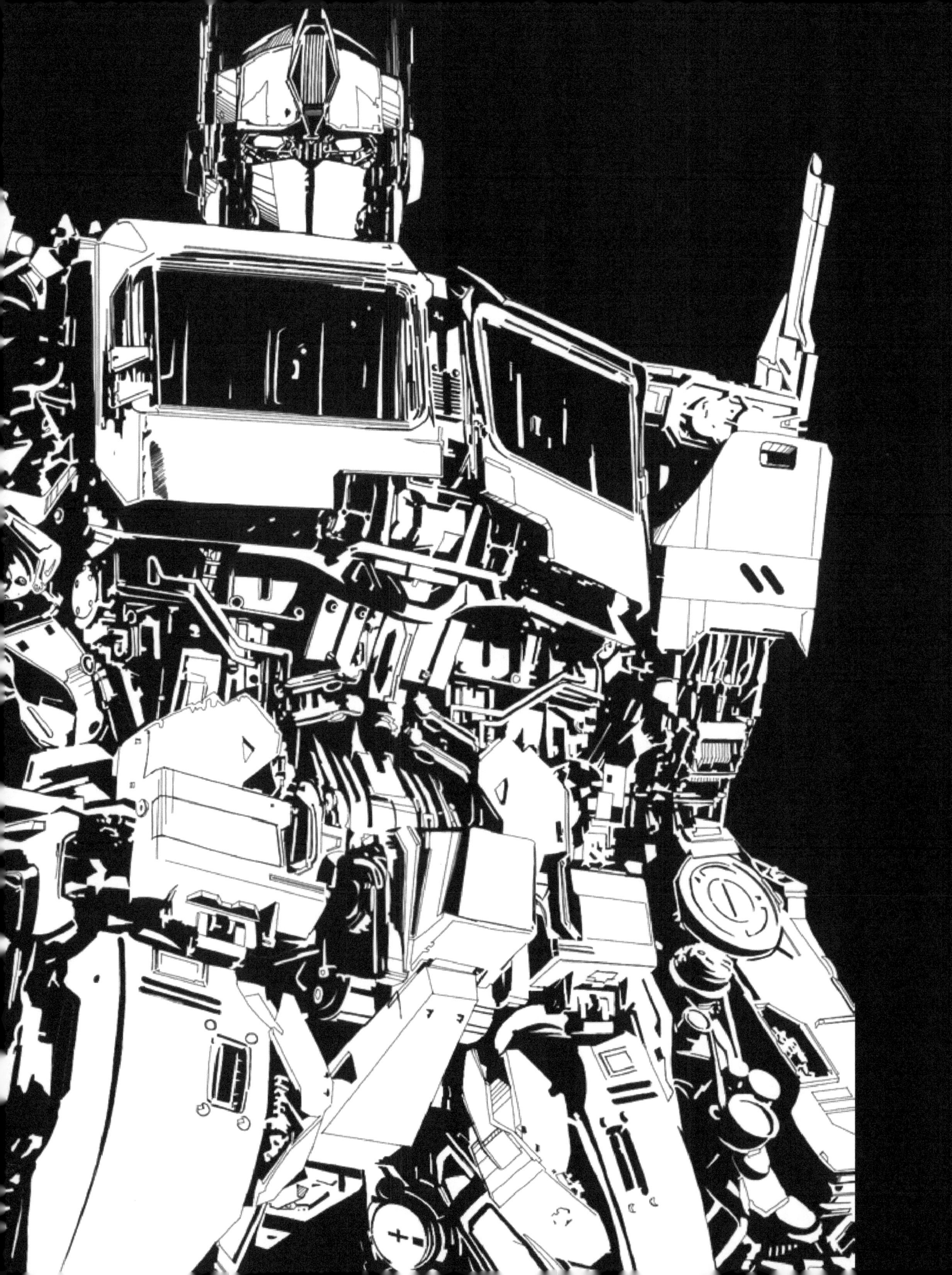

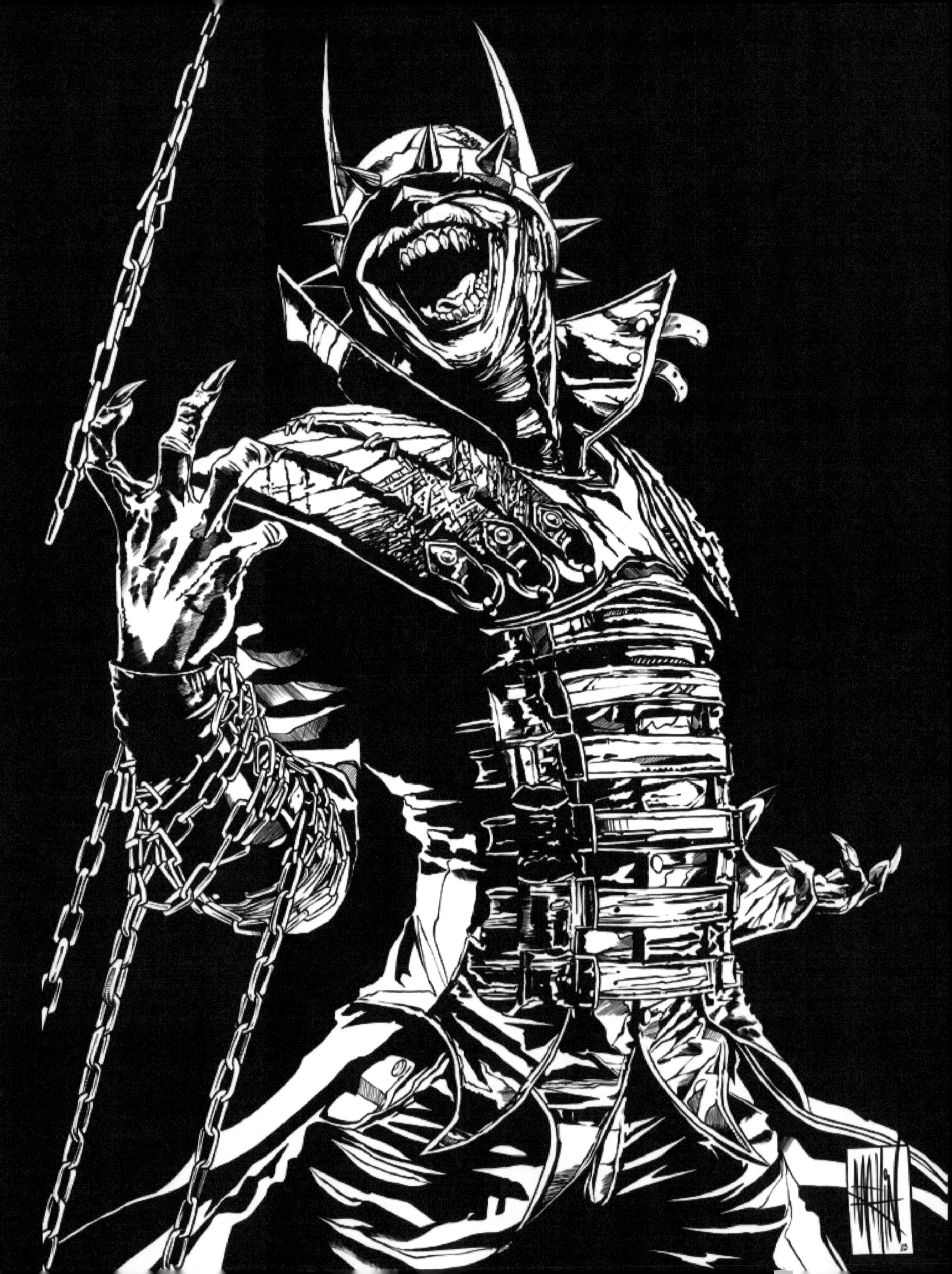

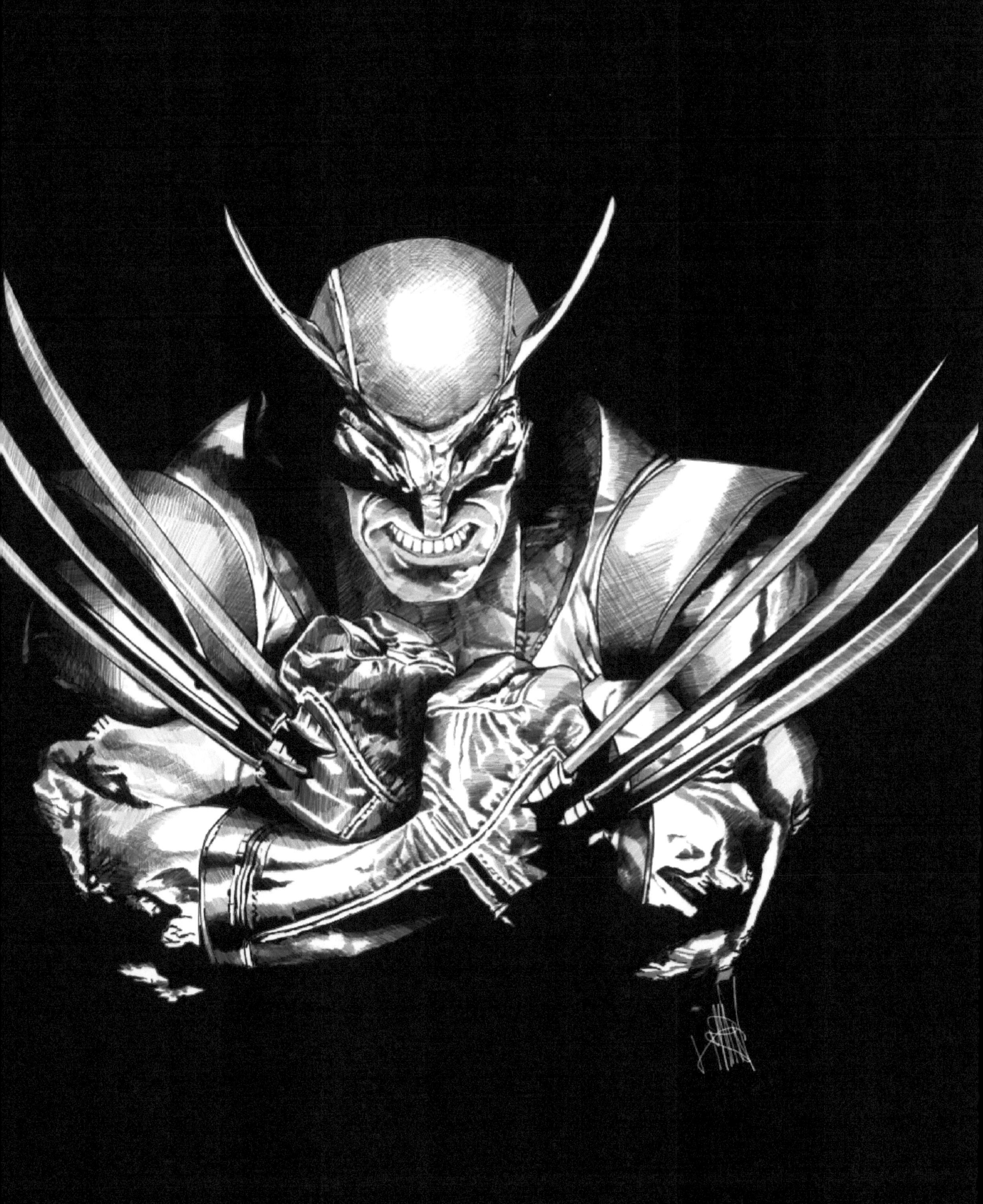

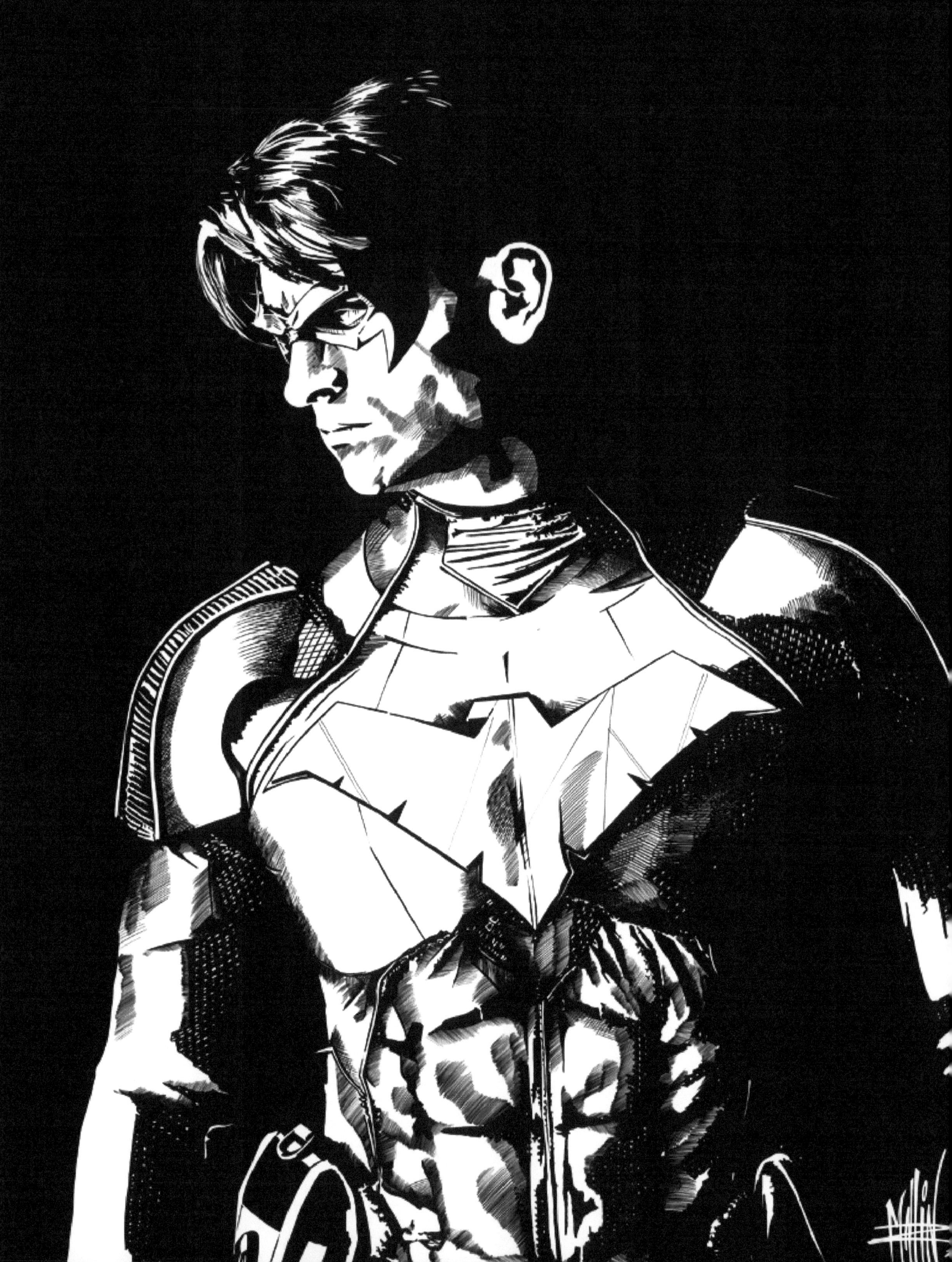

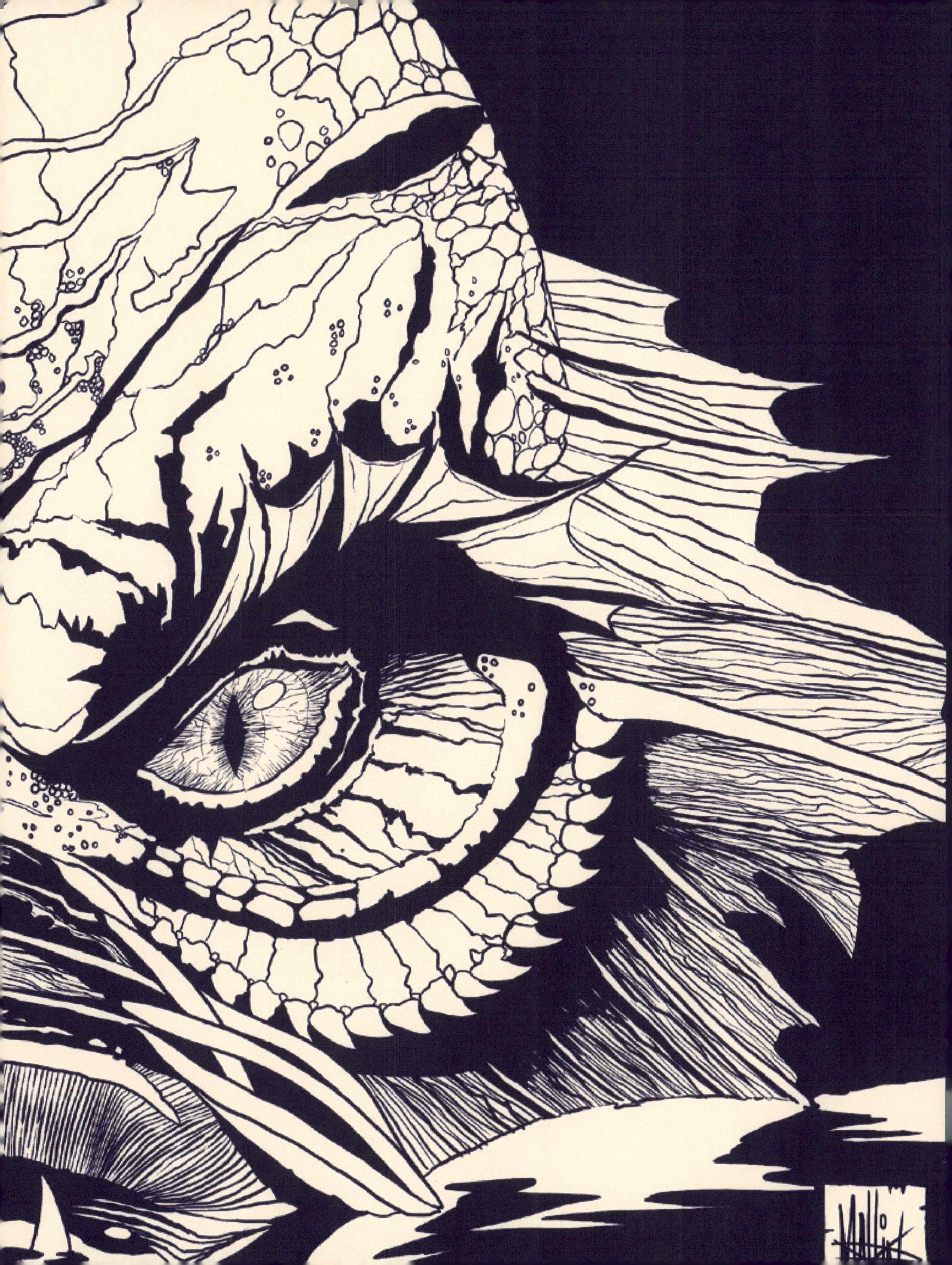

ボバ
フェット

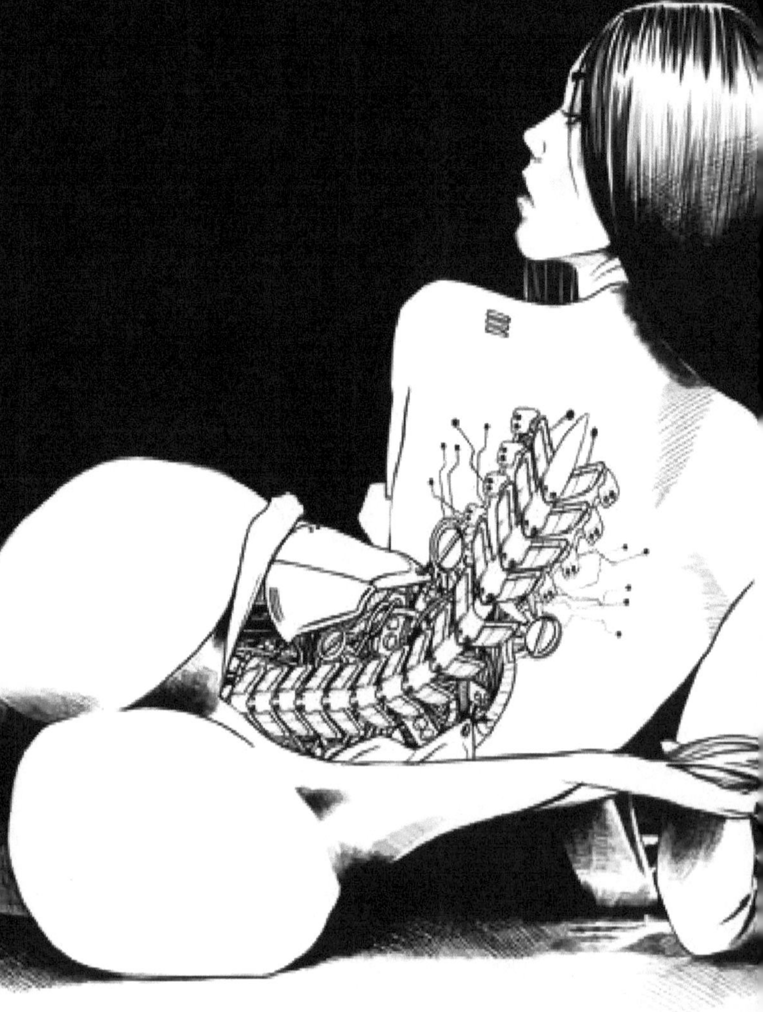

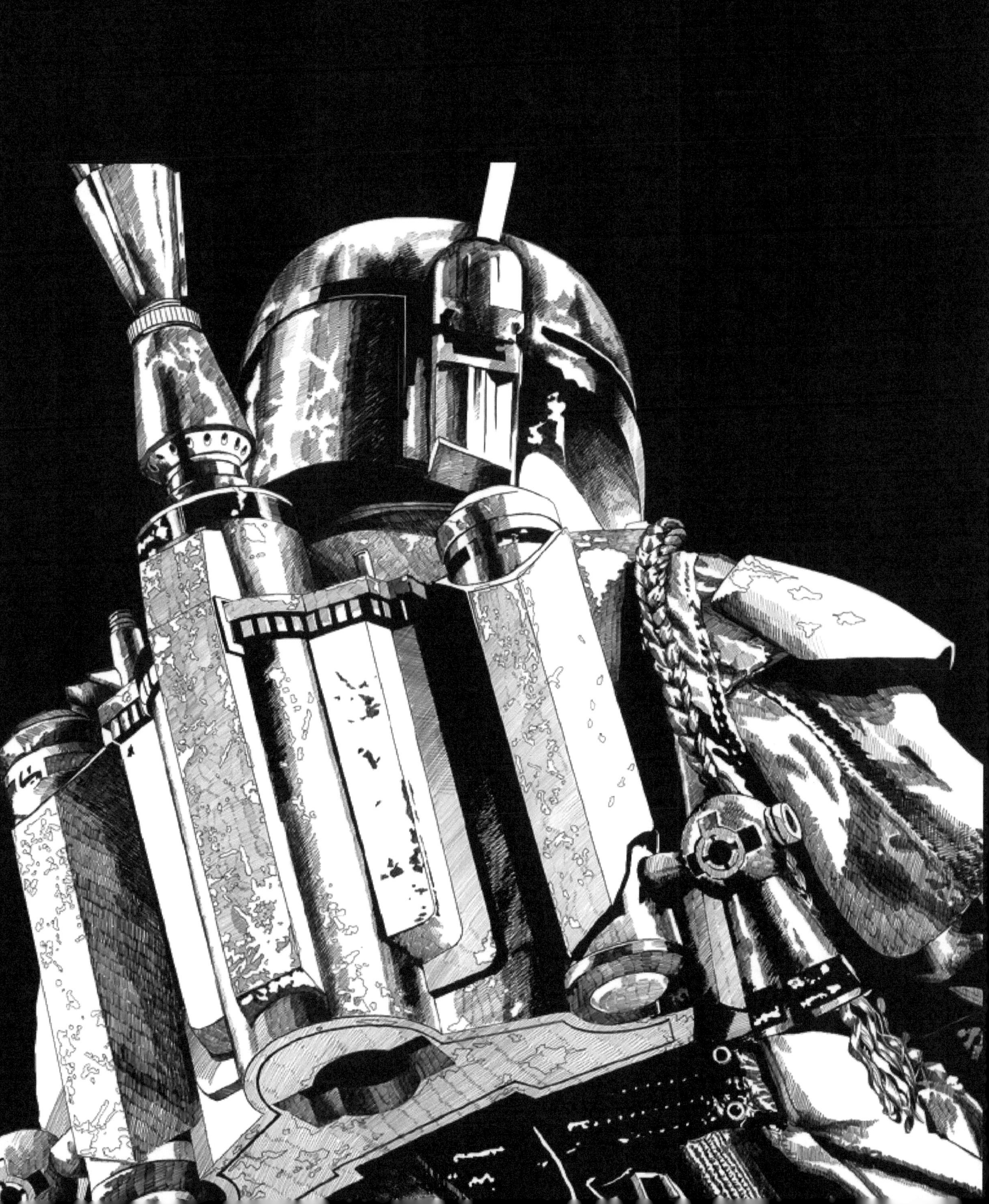

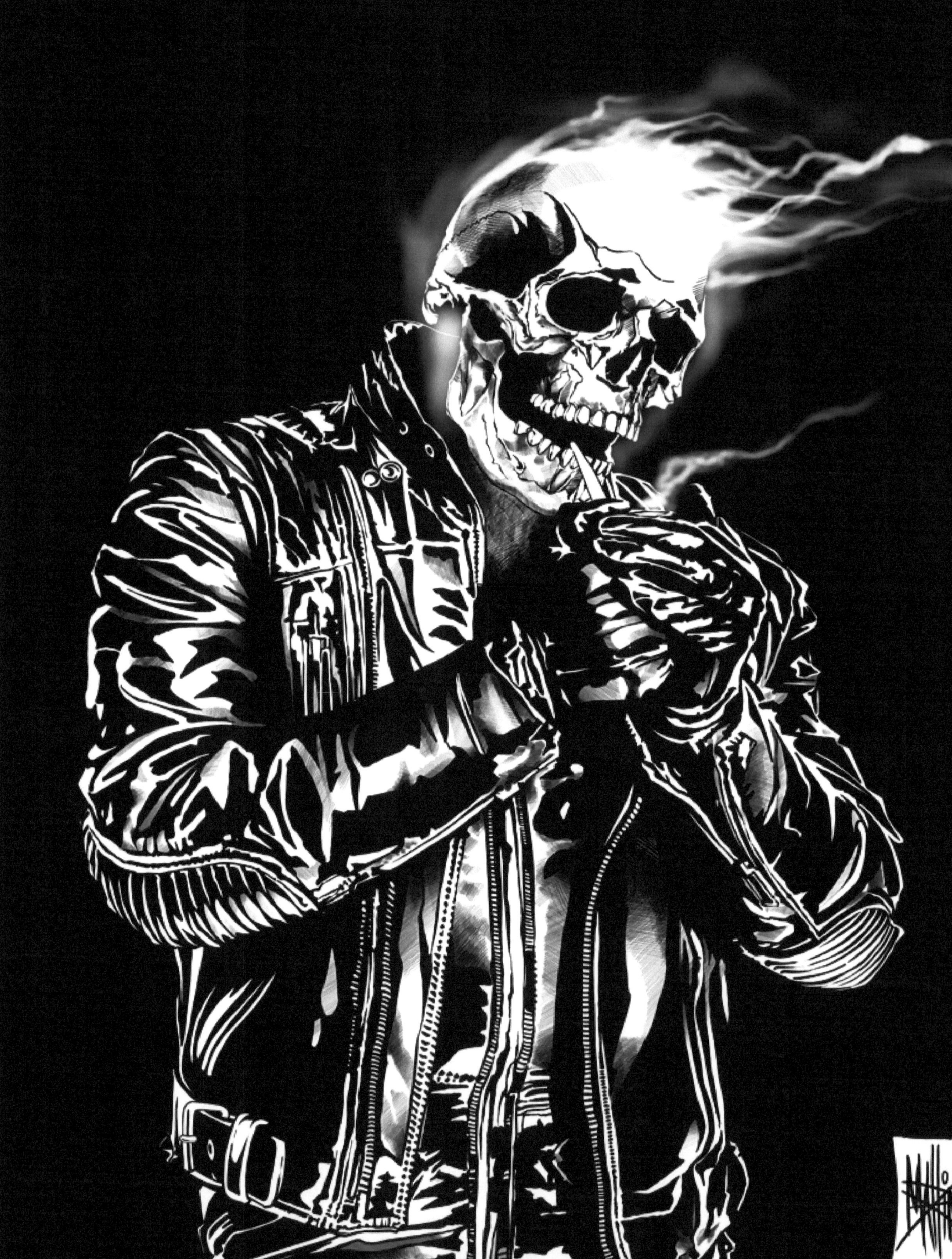

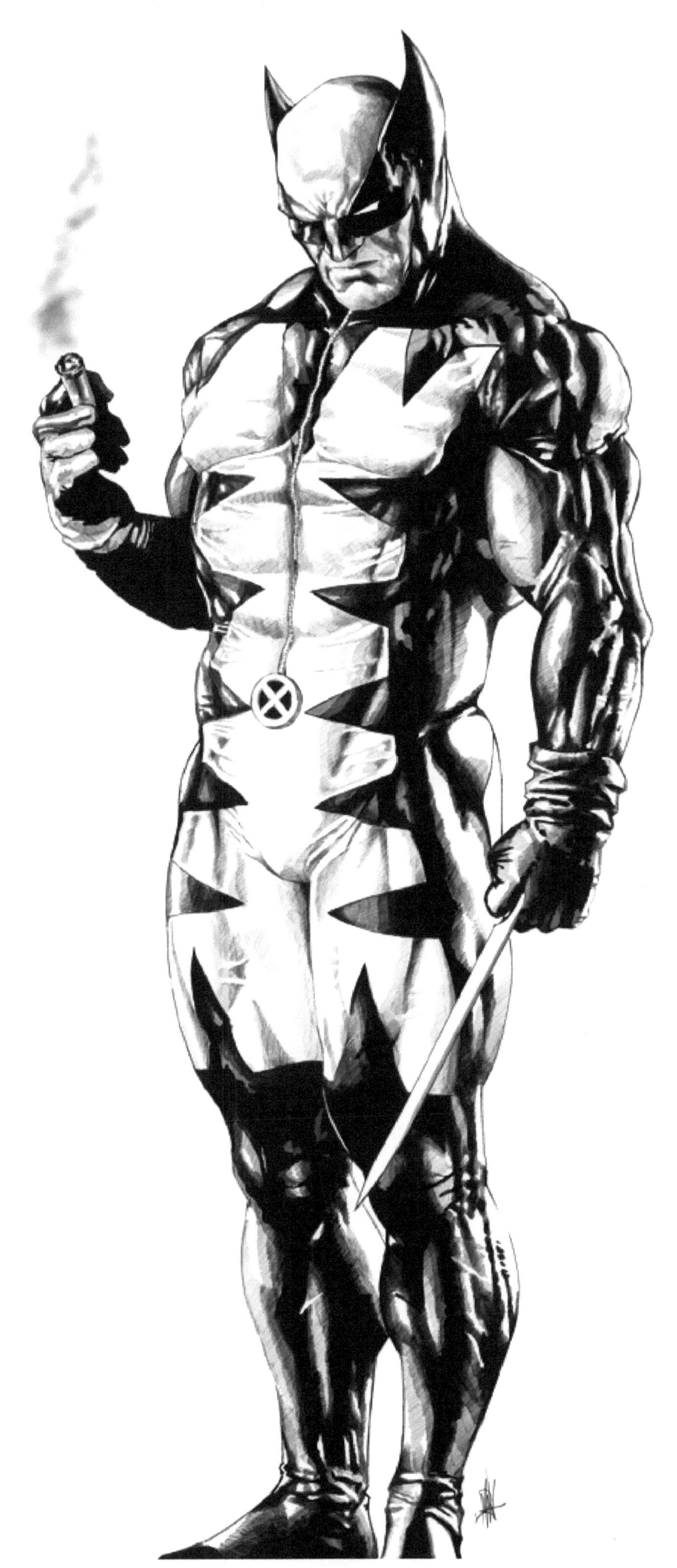

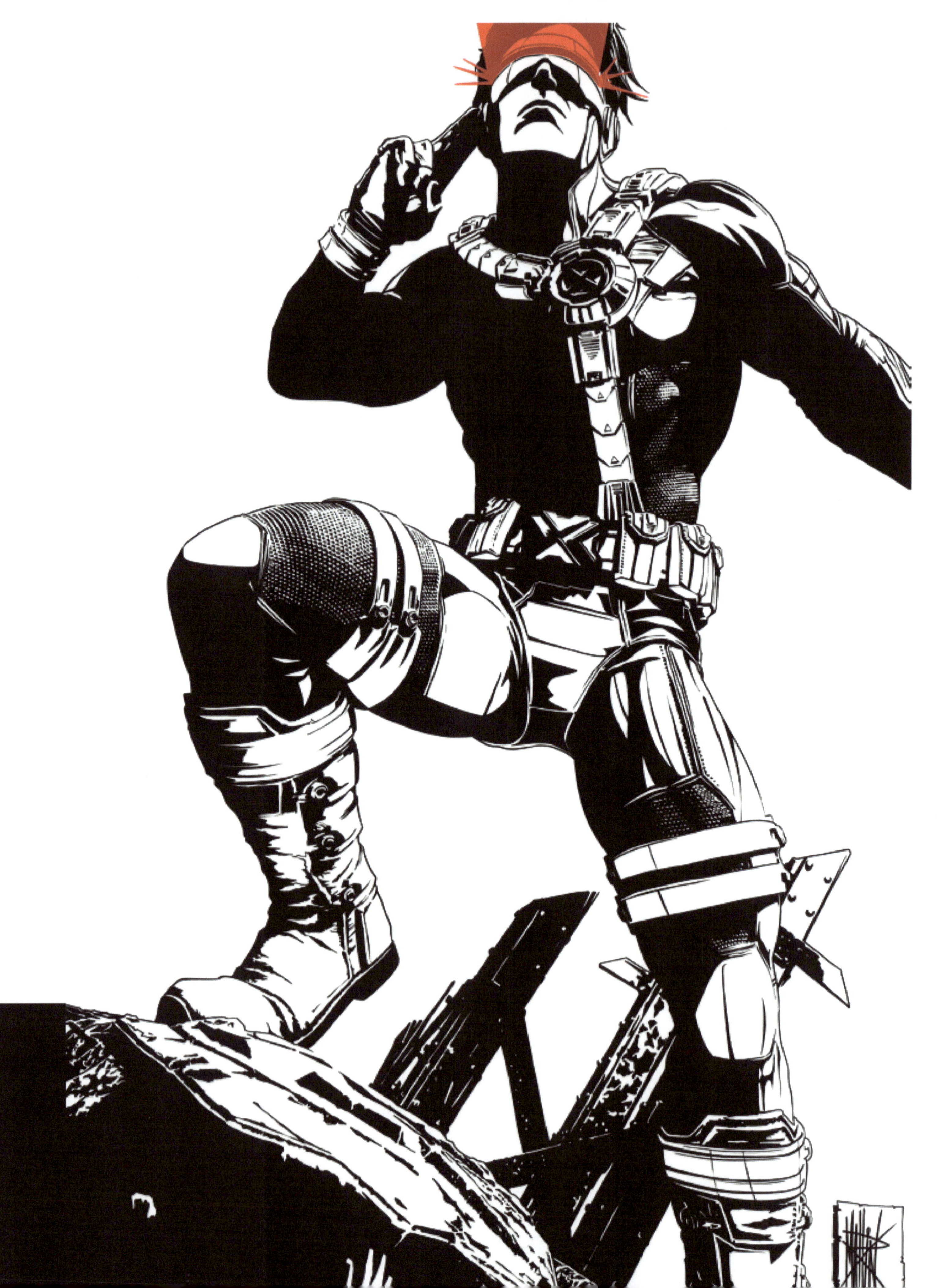

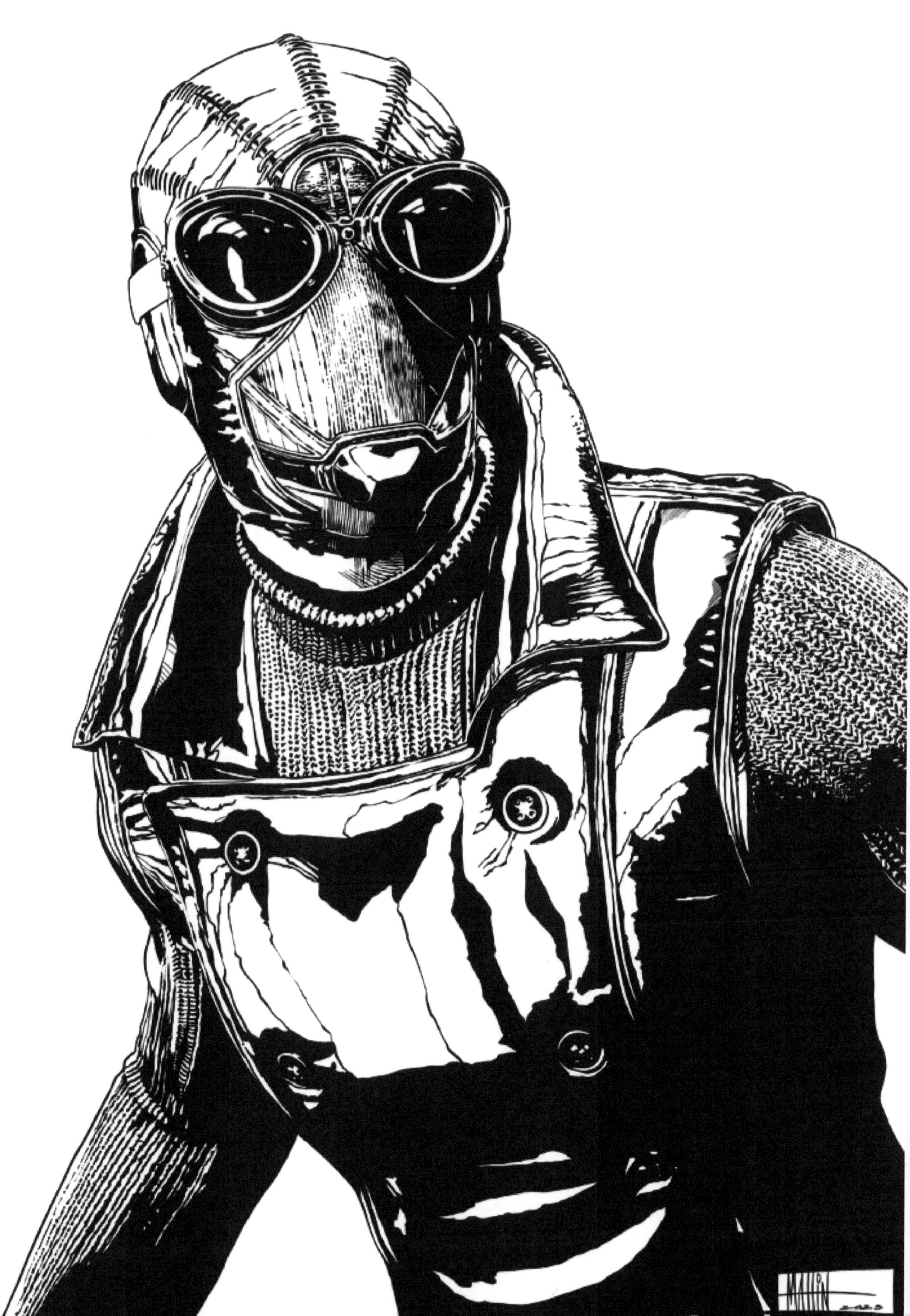

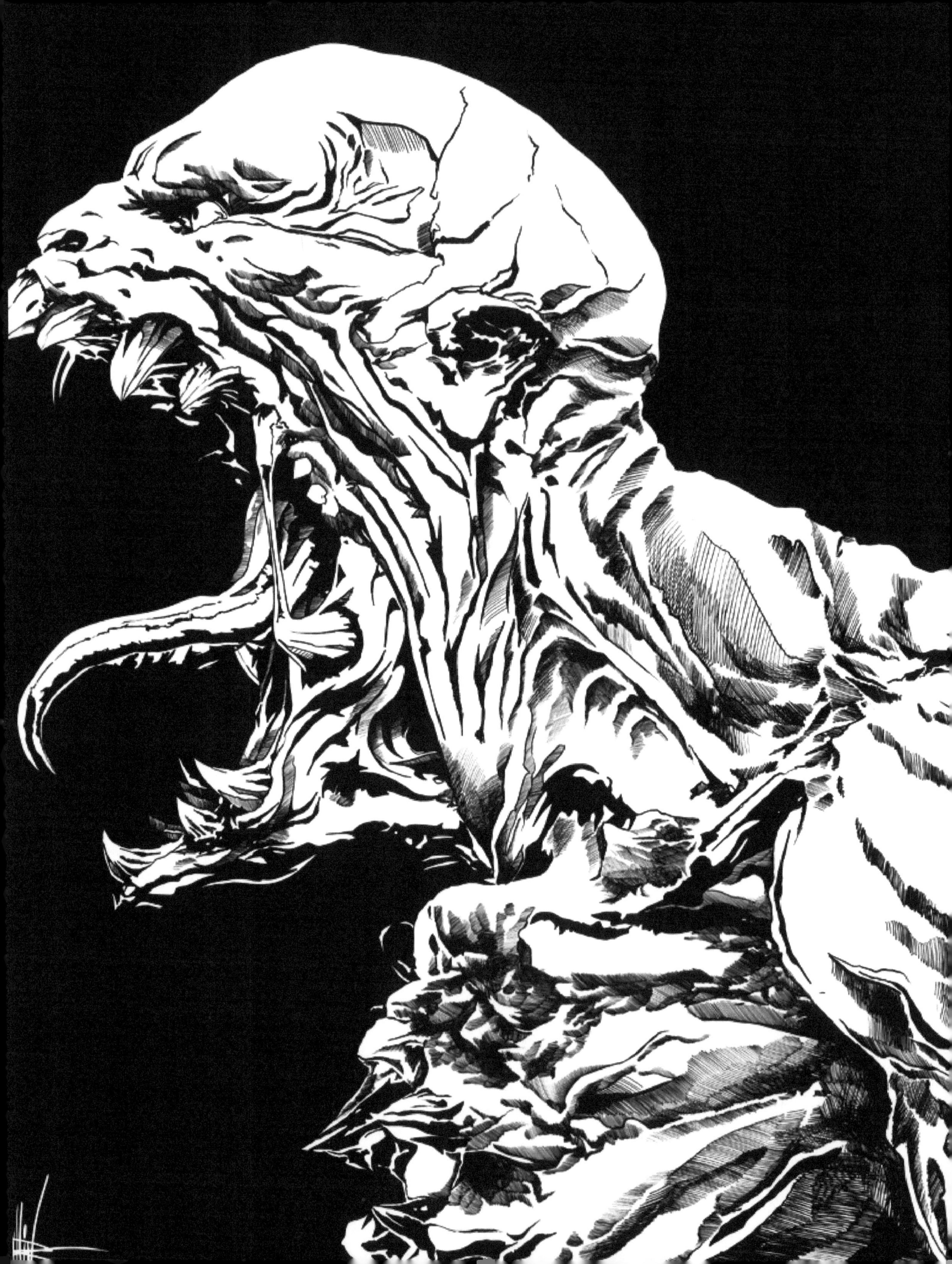

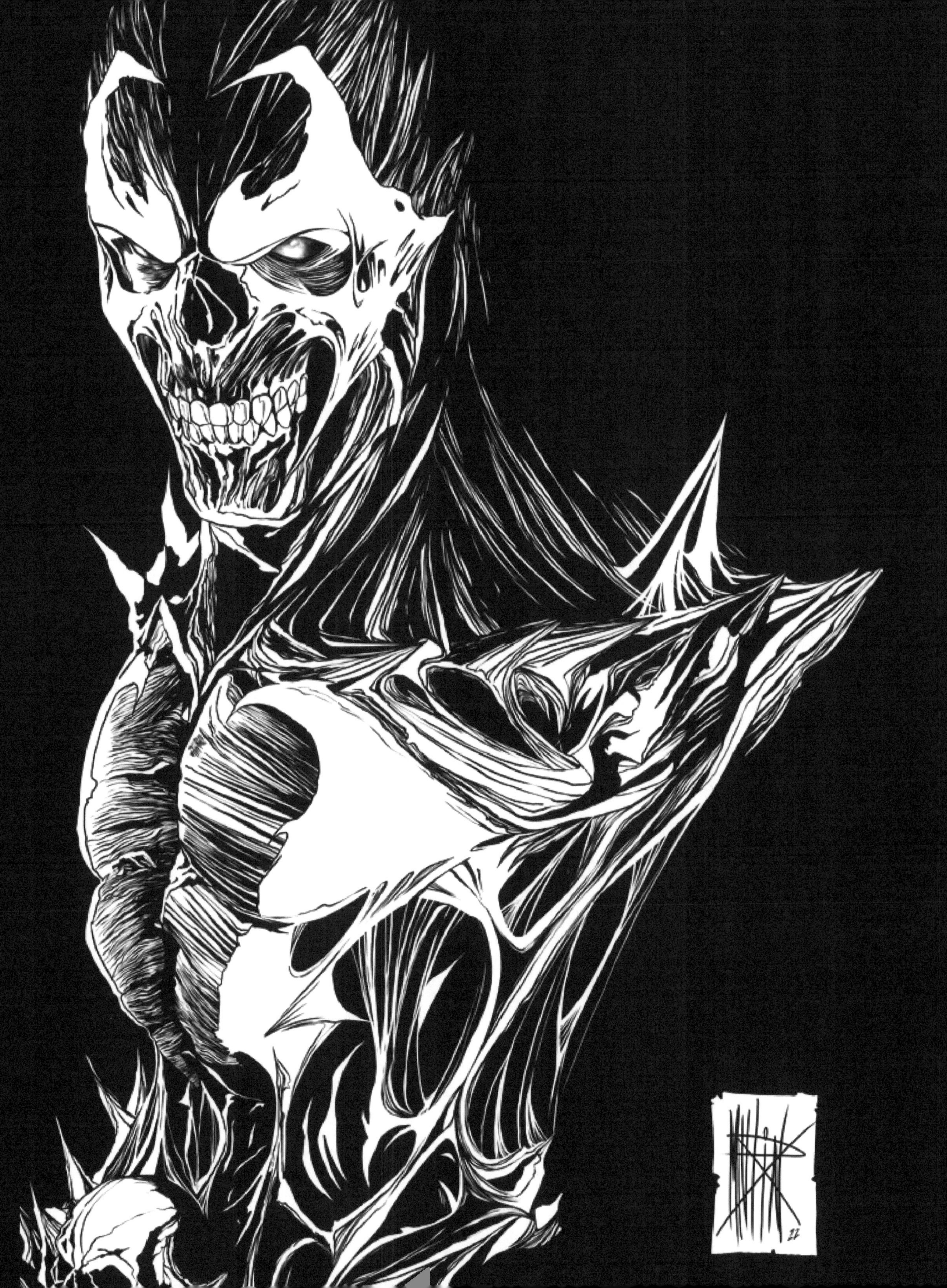

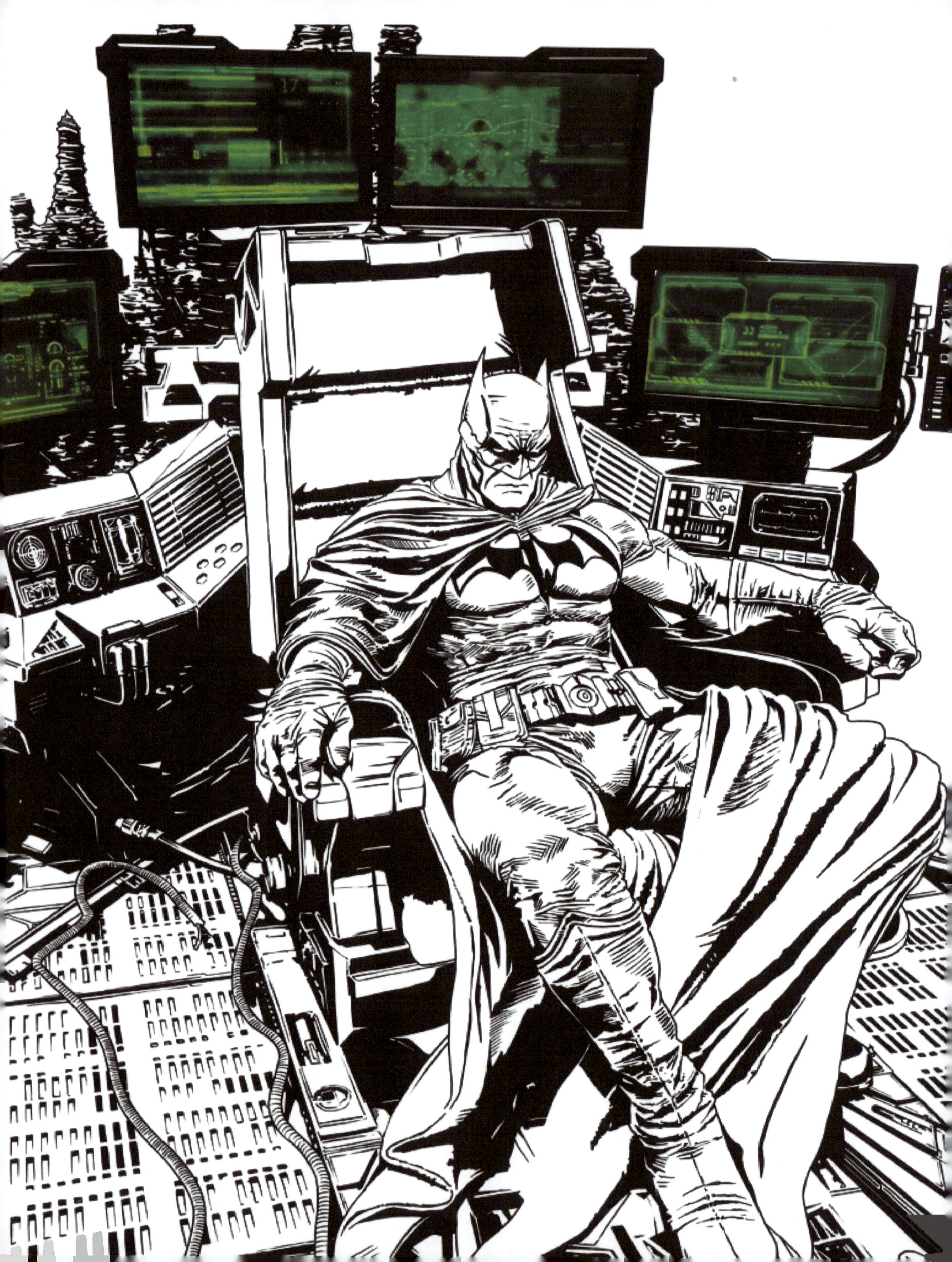

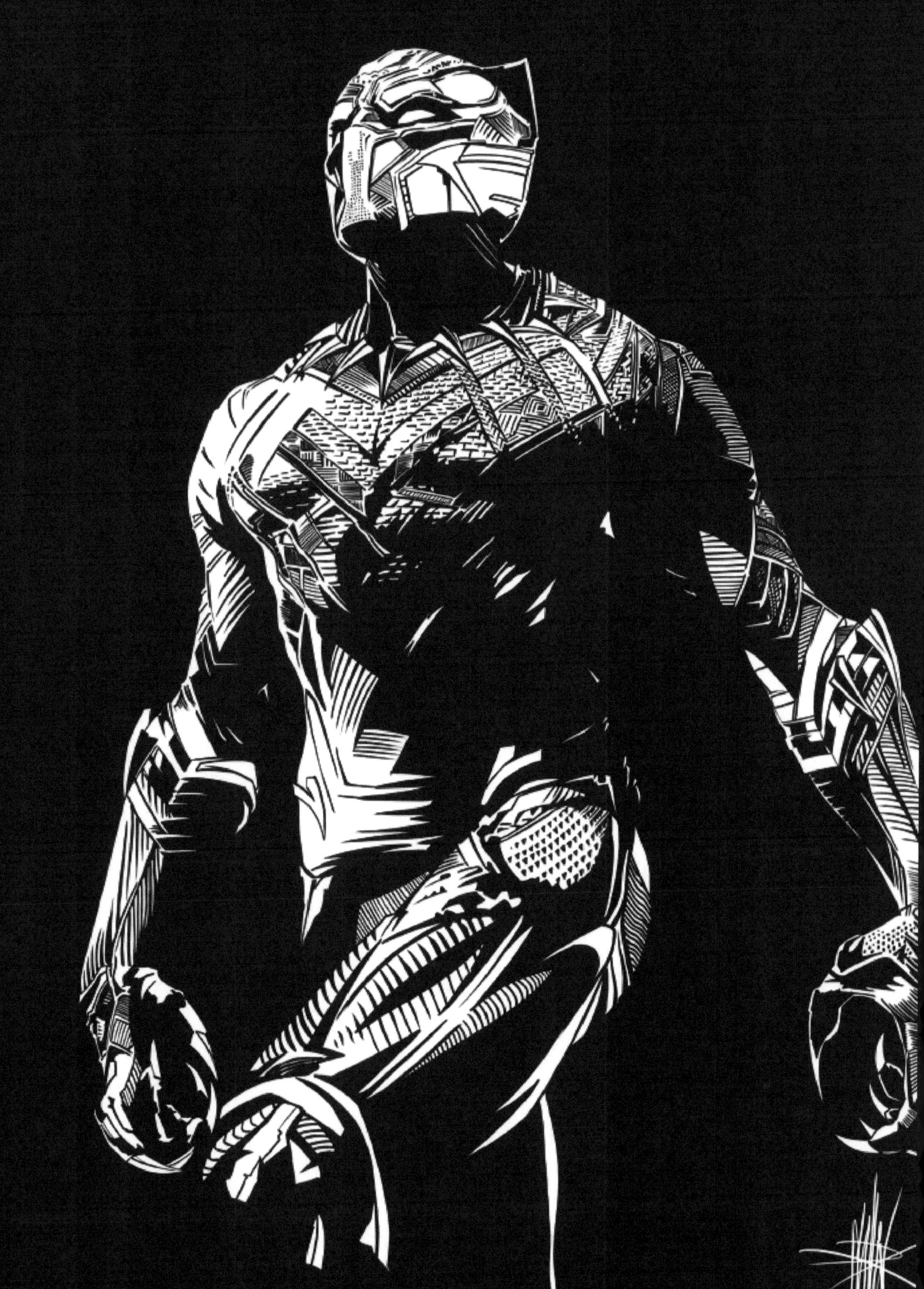

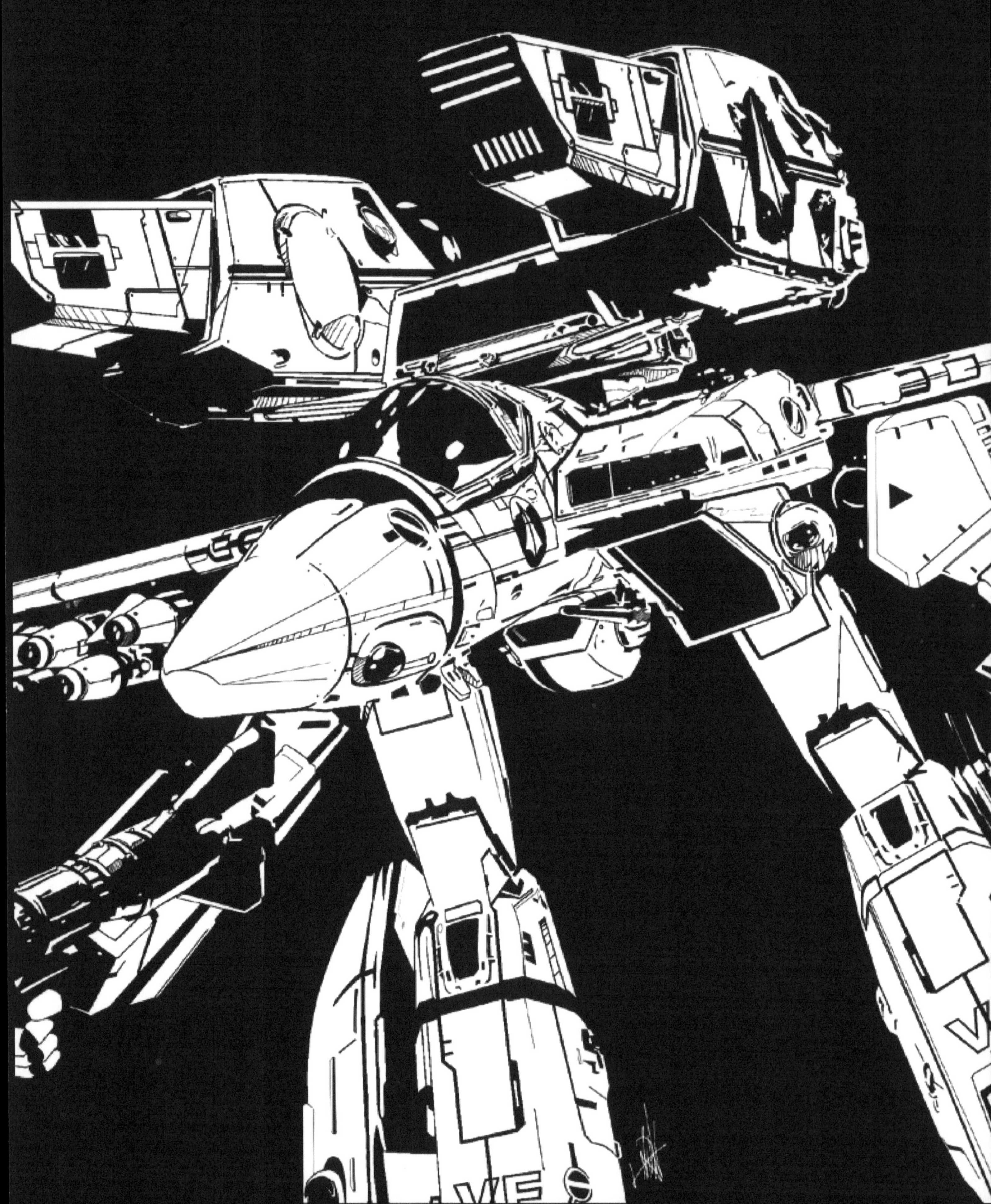

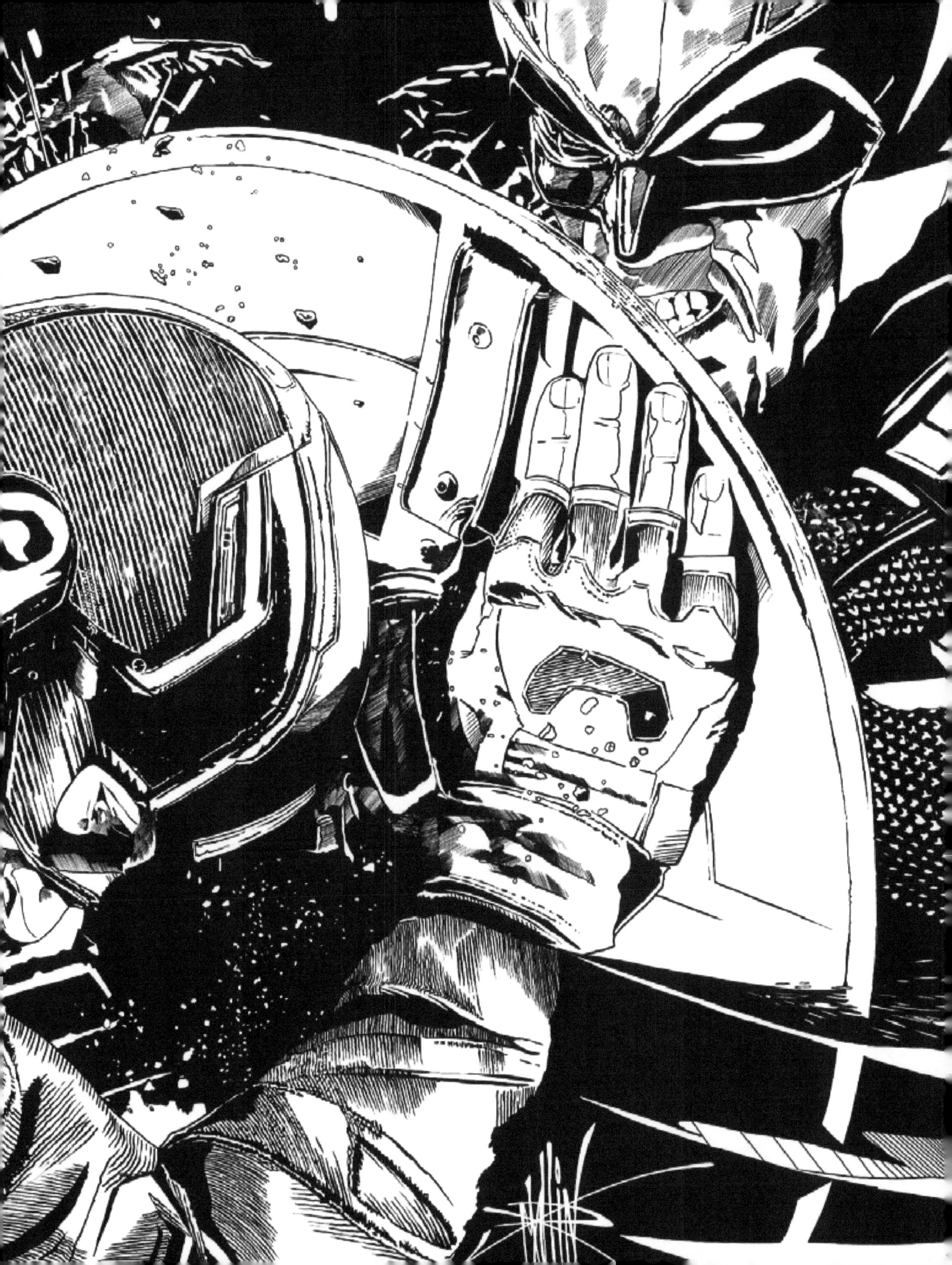

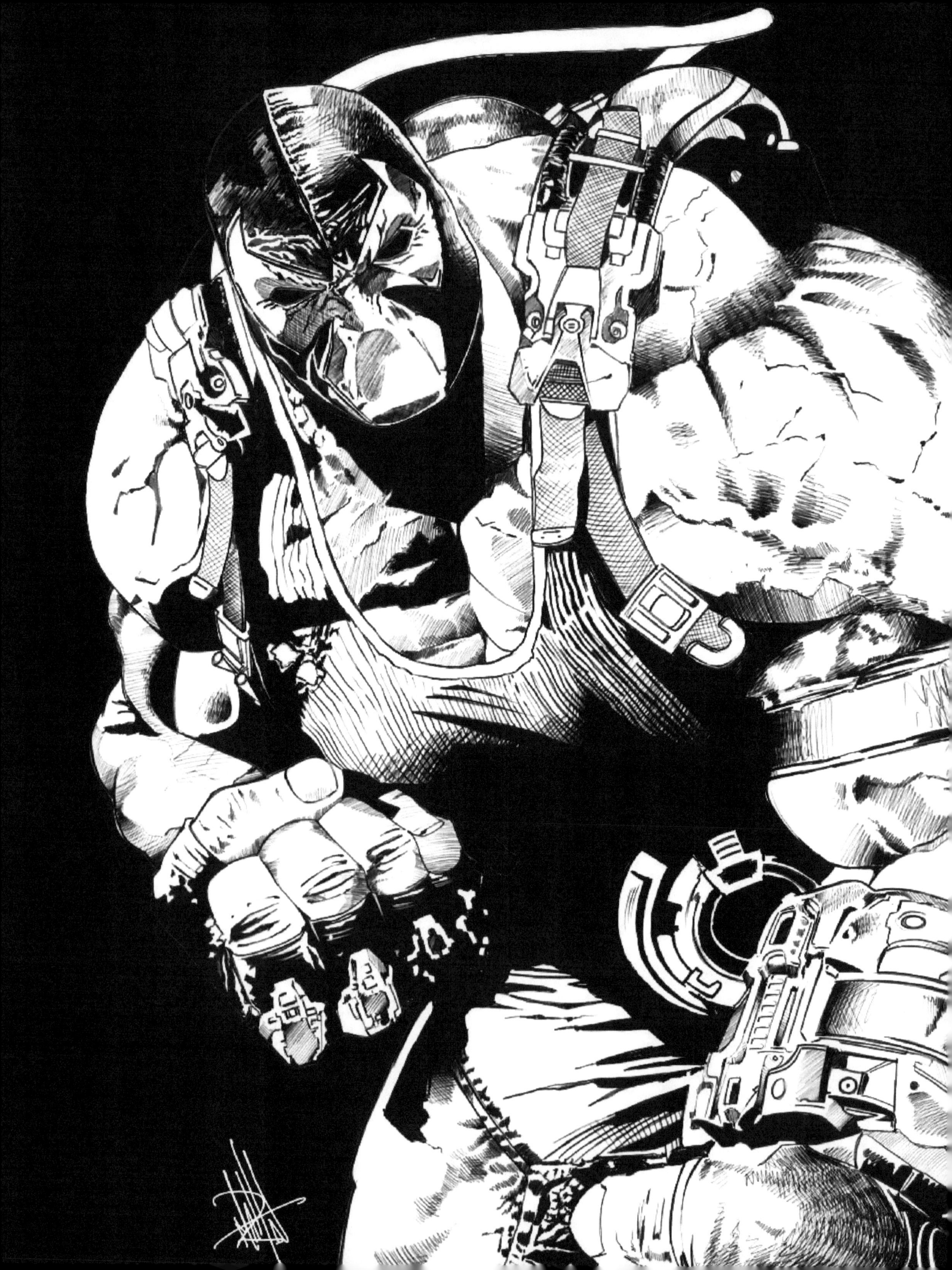

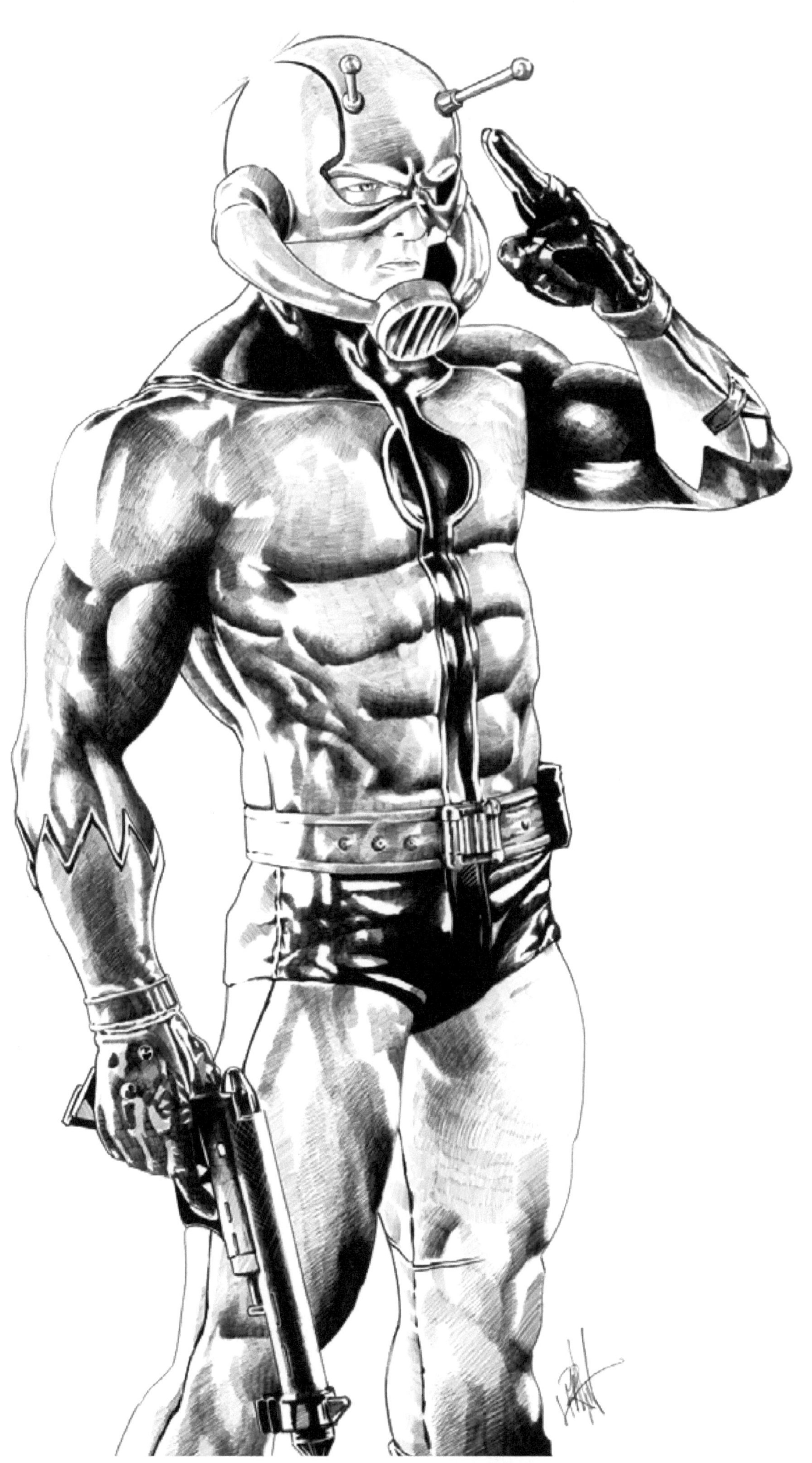

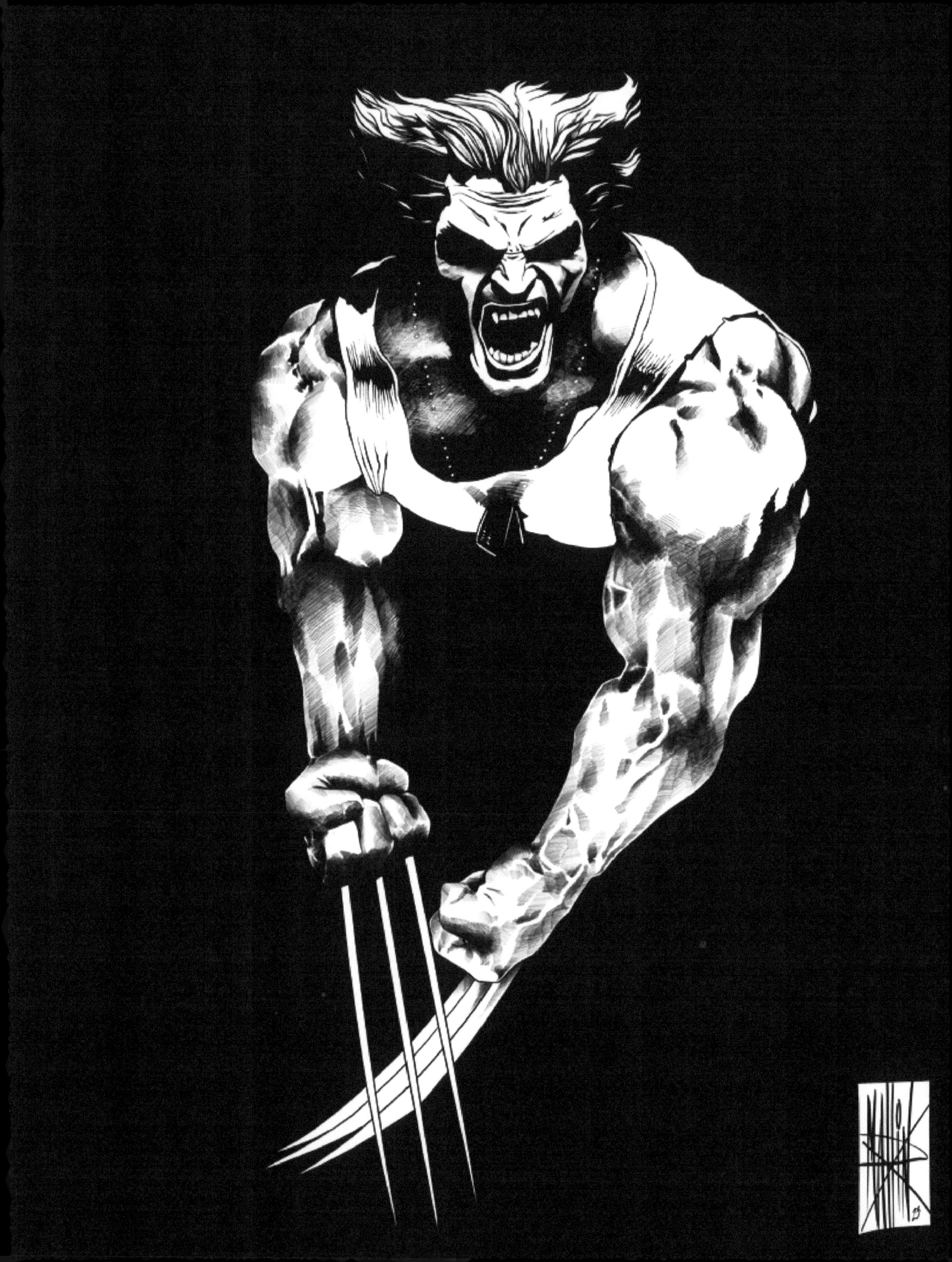

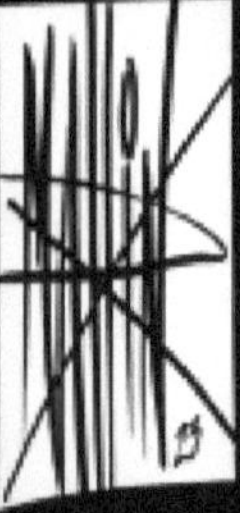

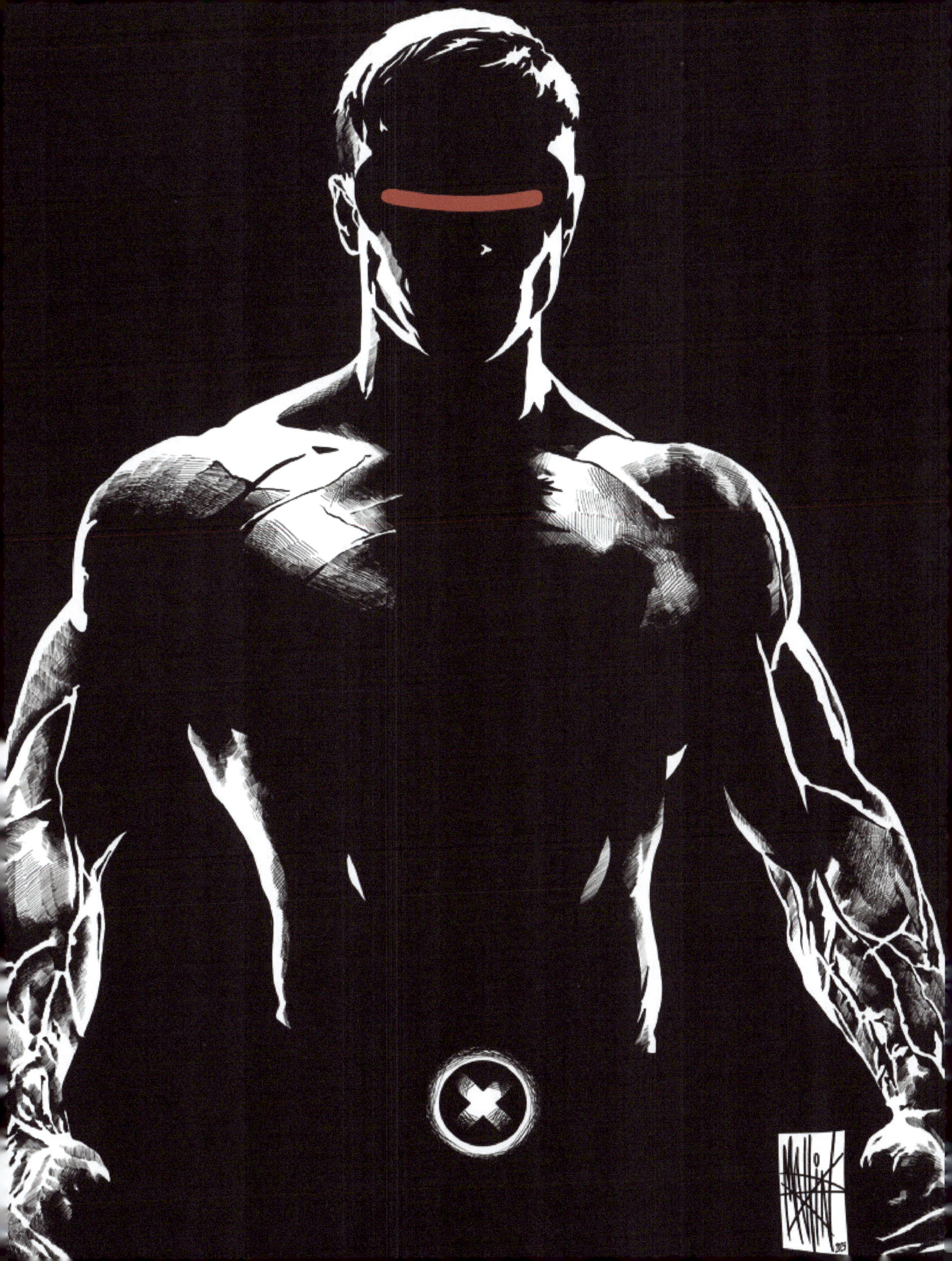

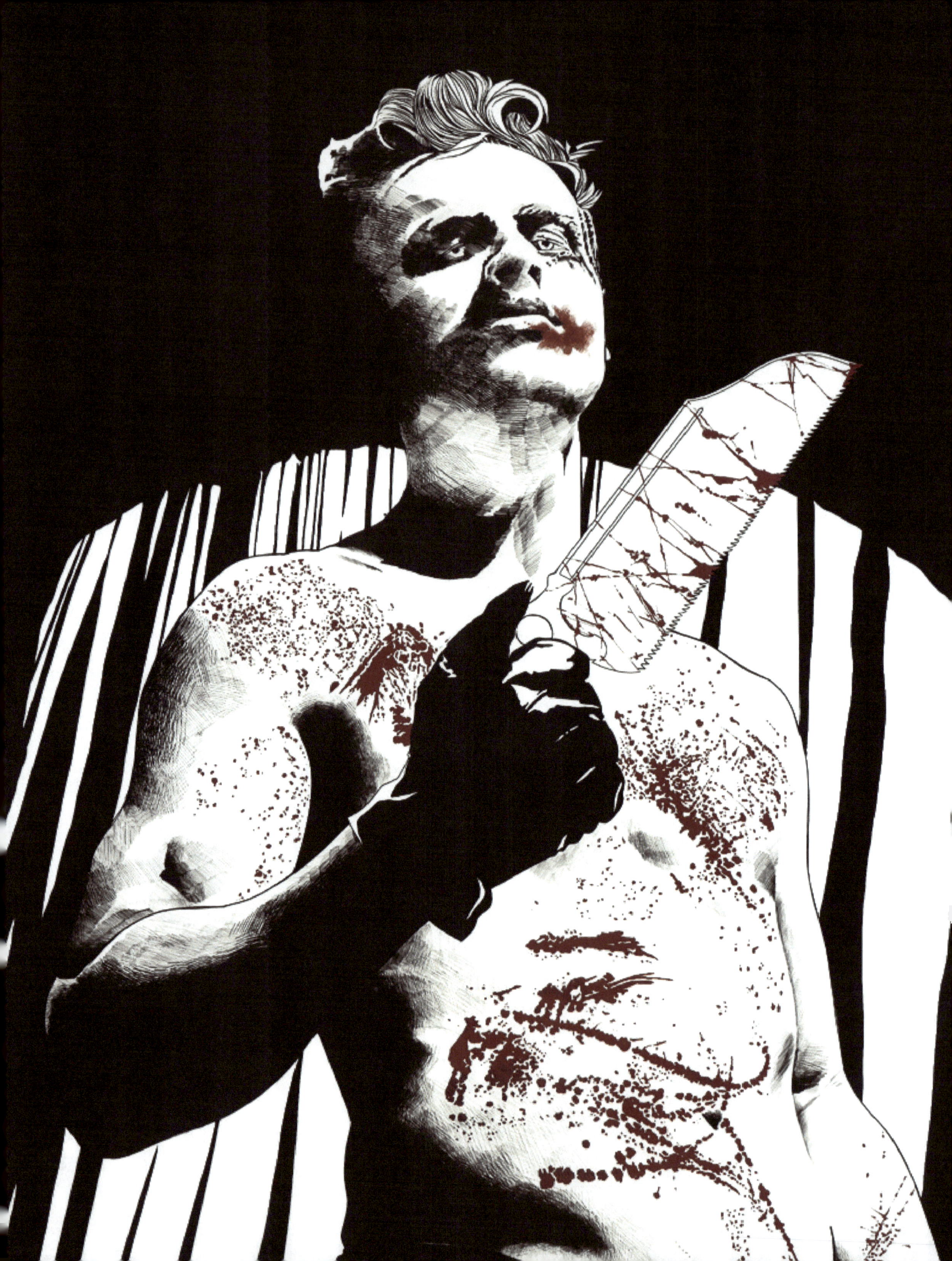

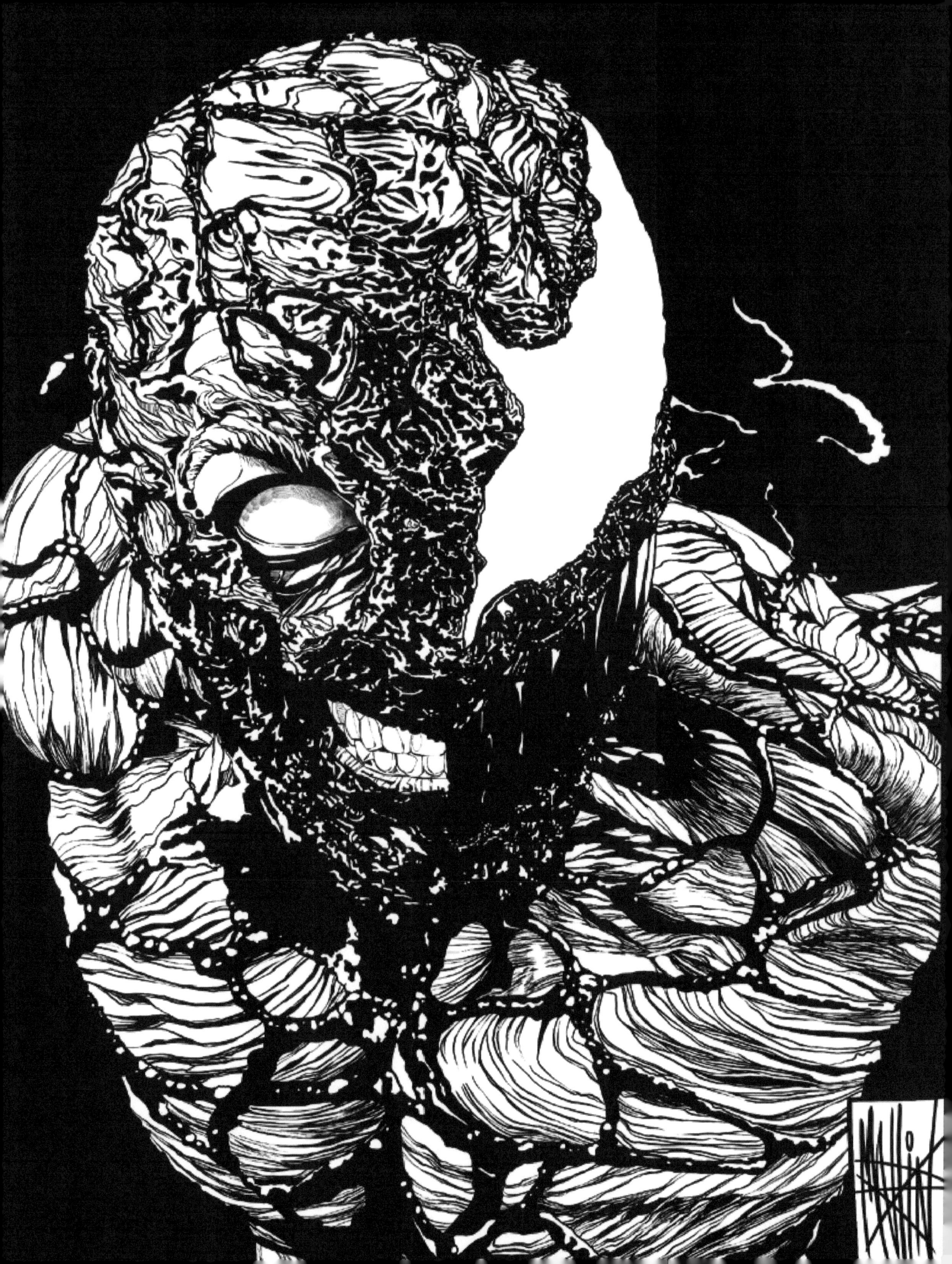

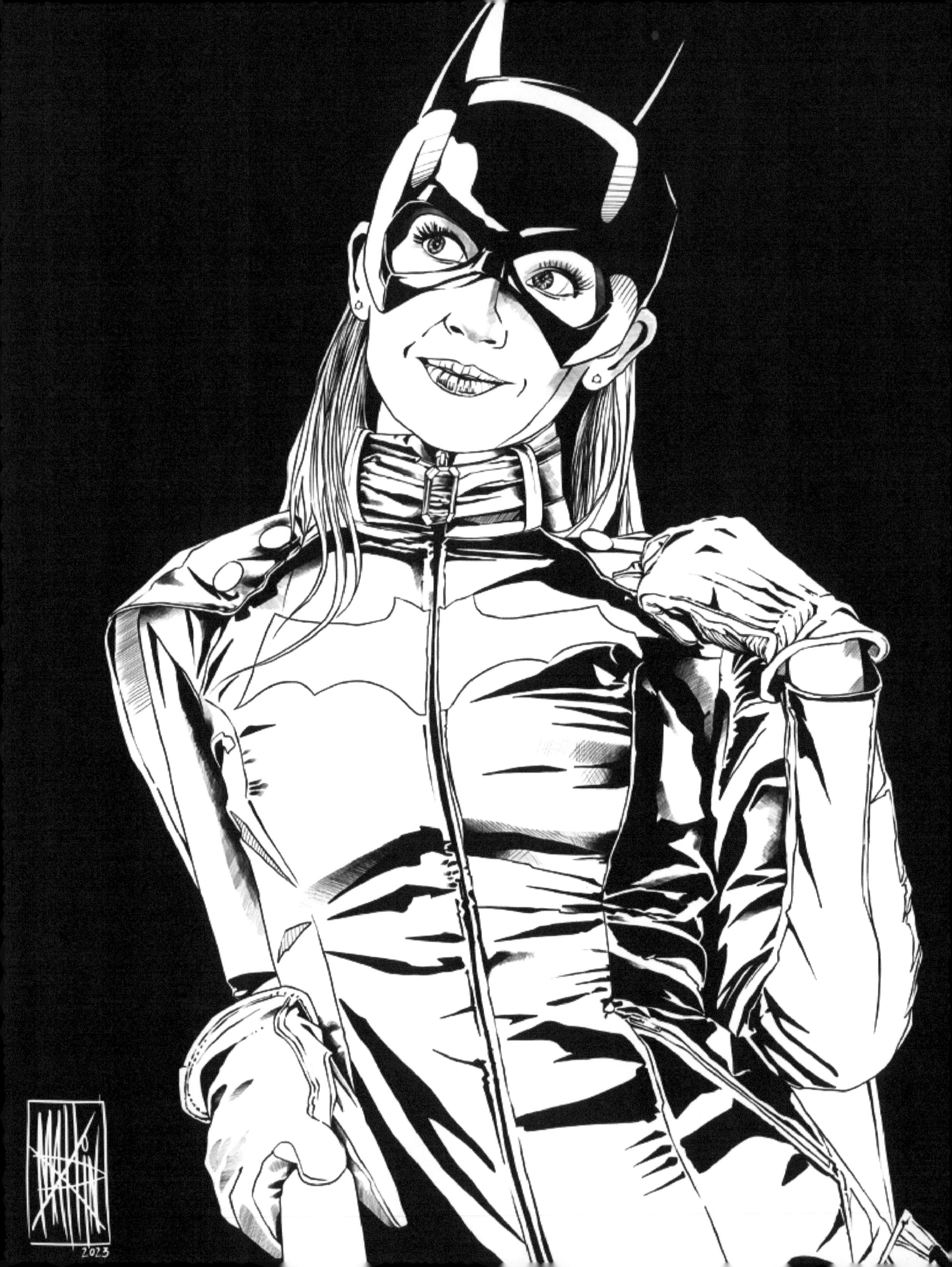

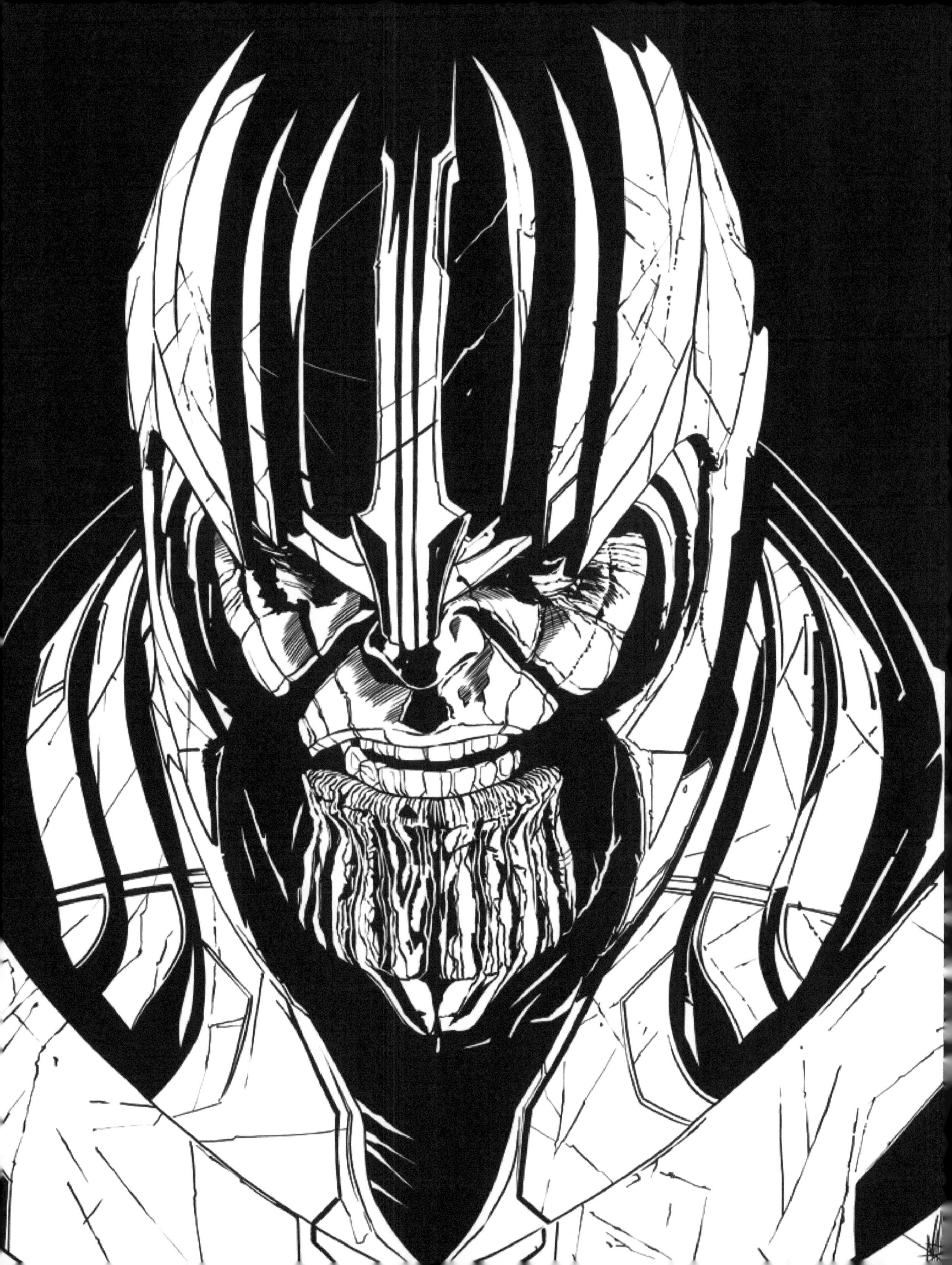

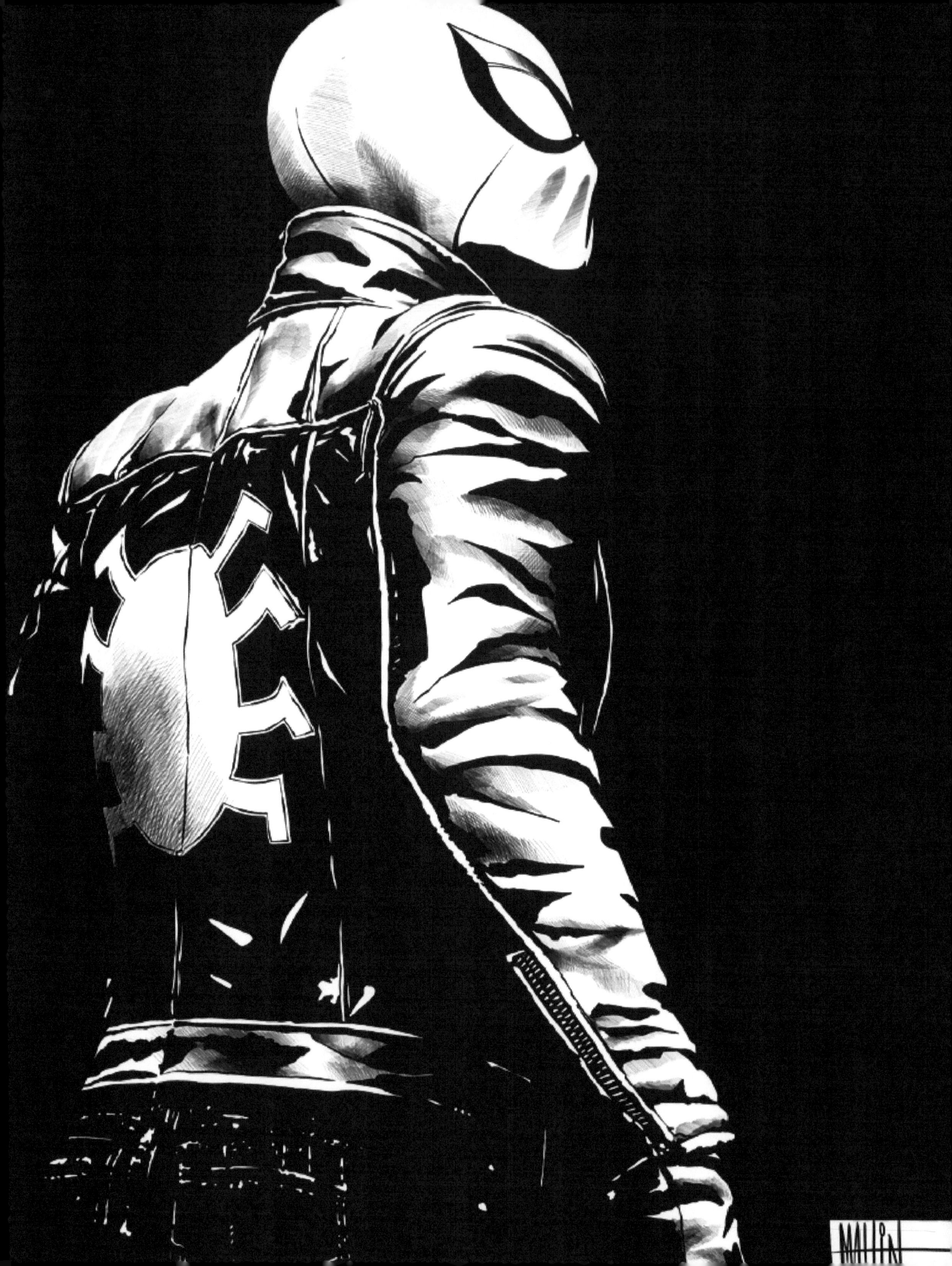

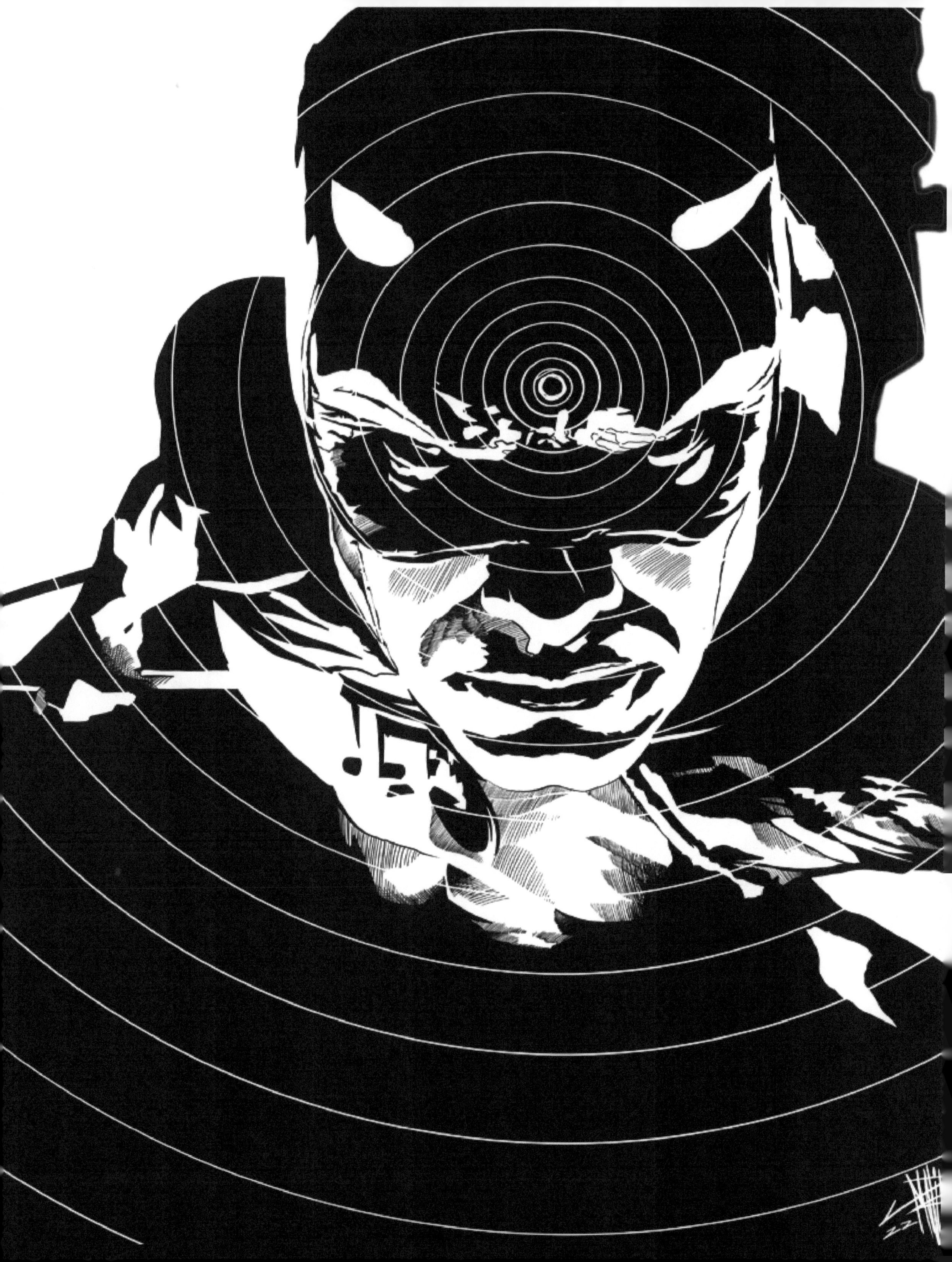

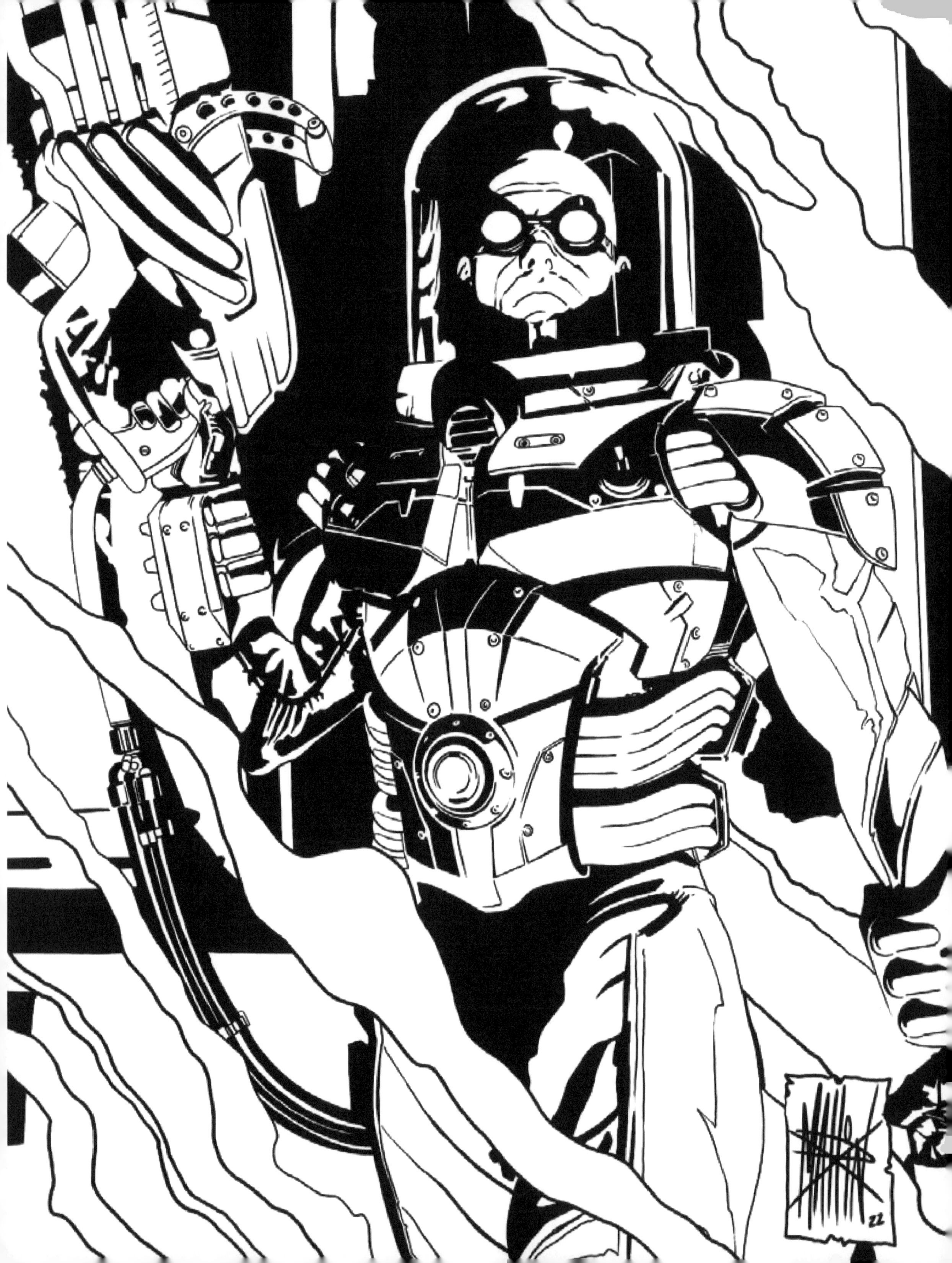

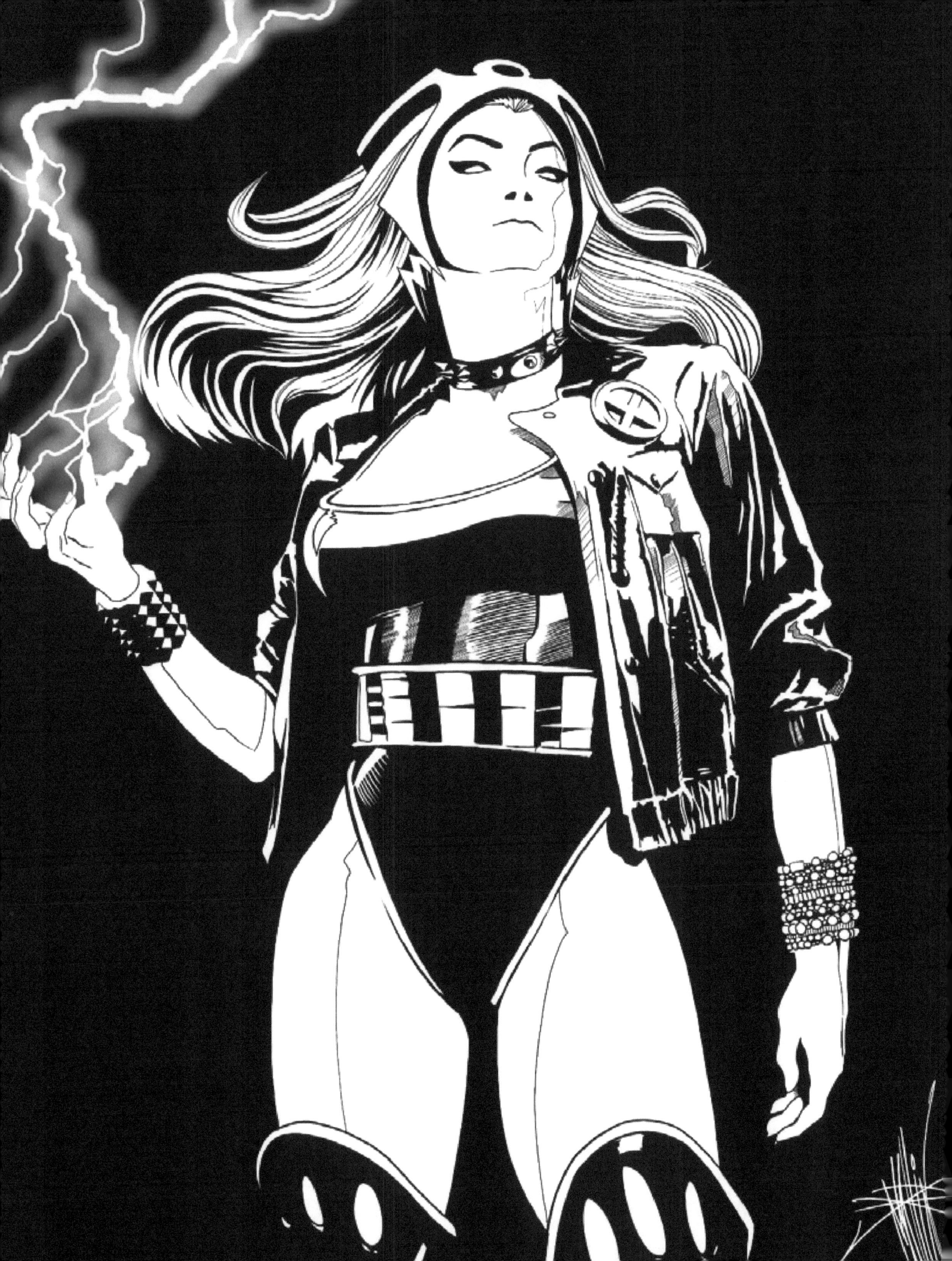

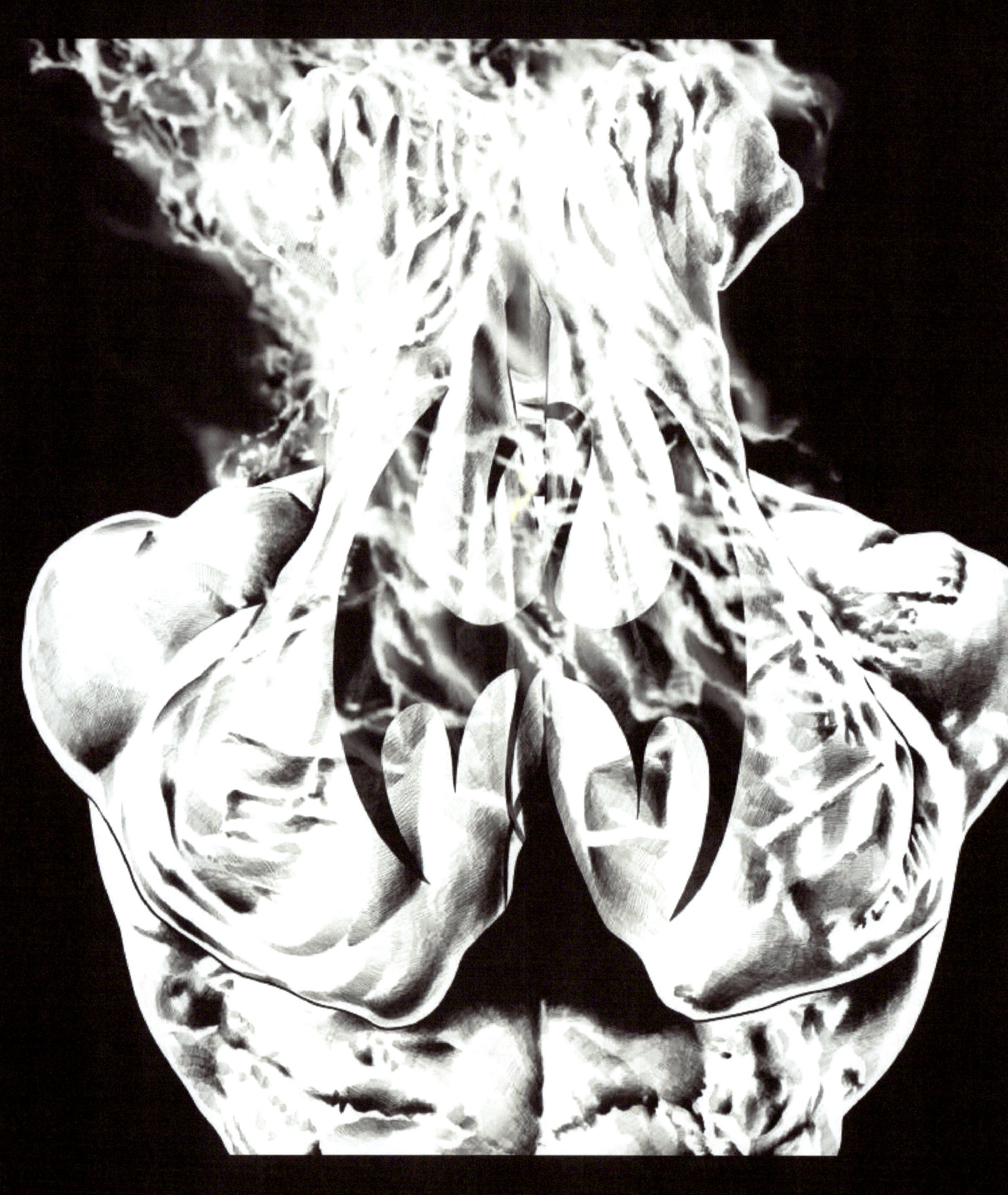

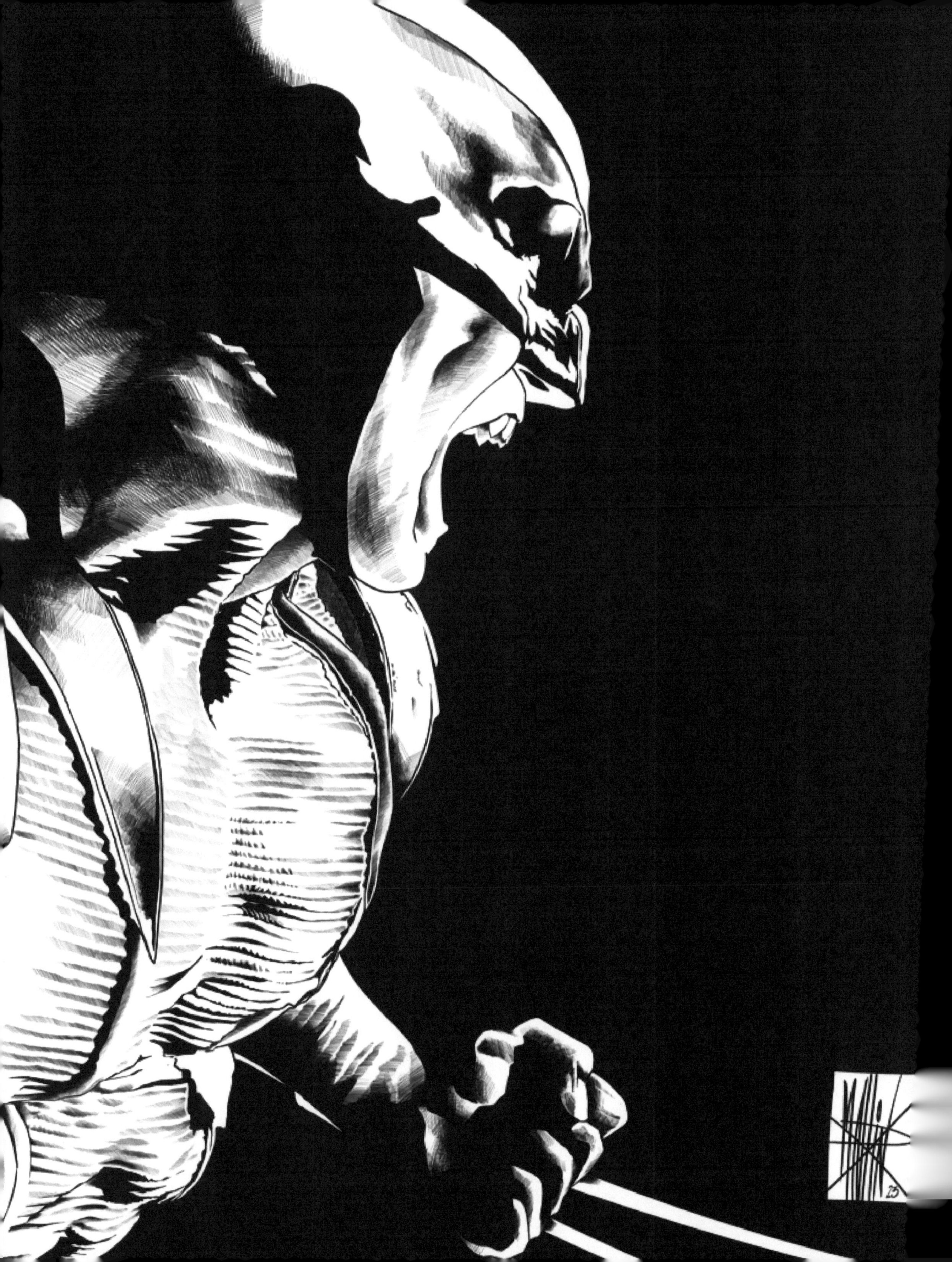

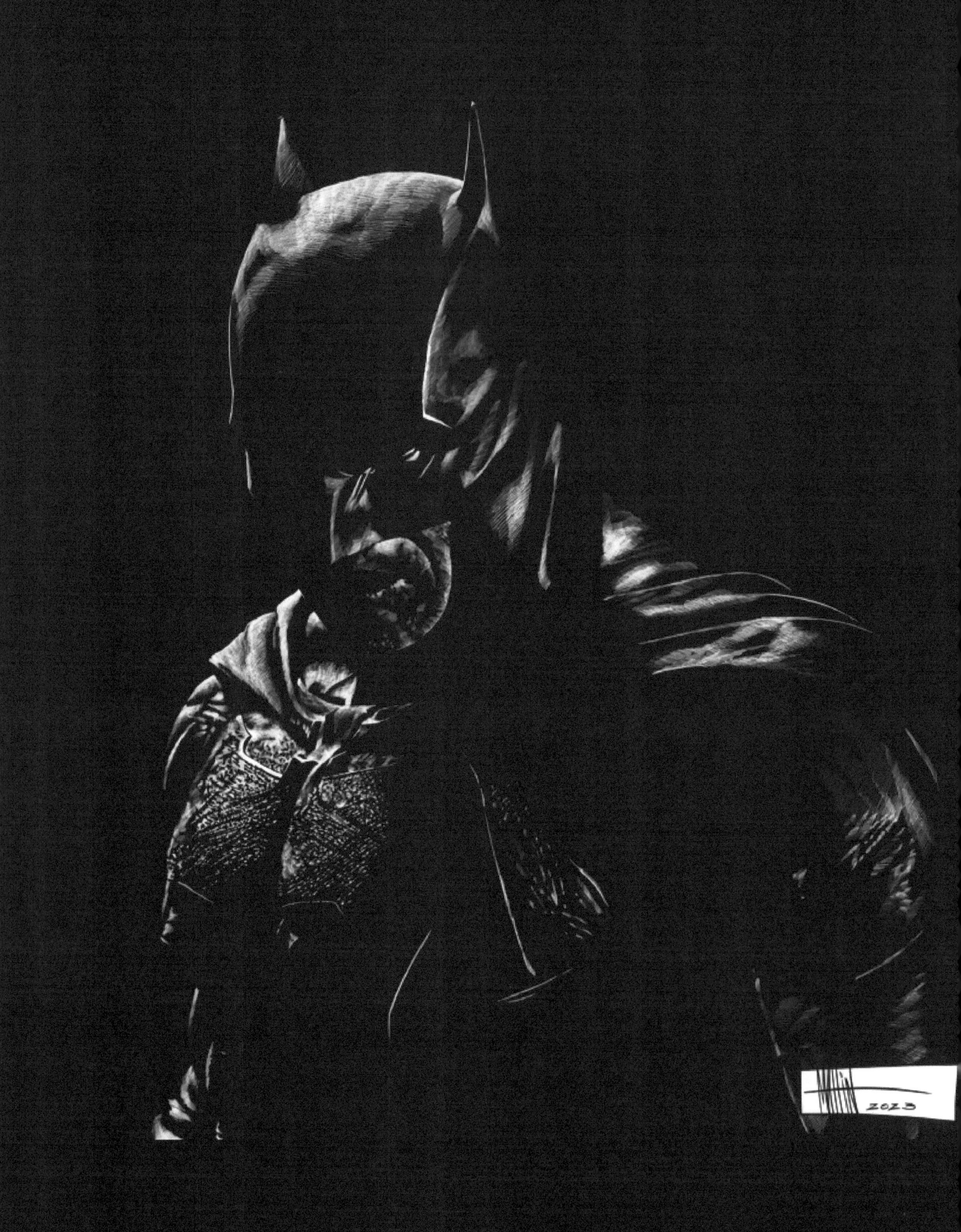

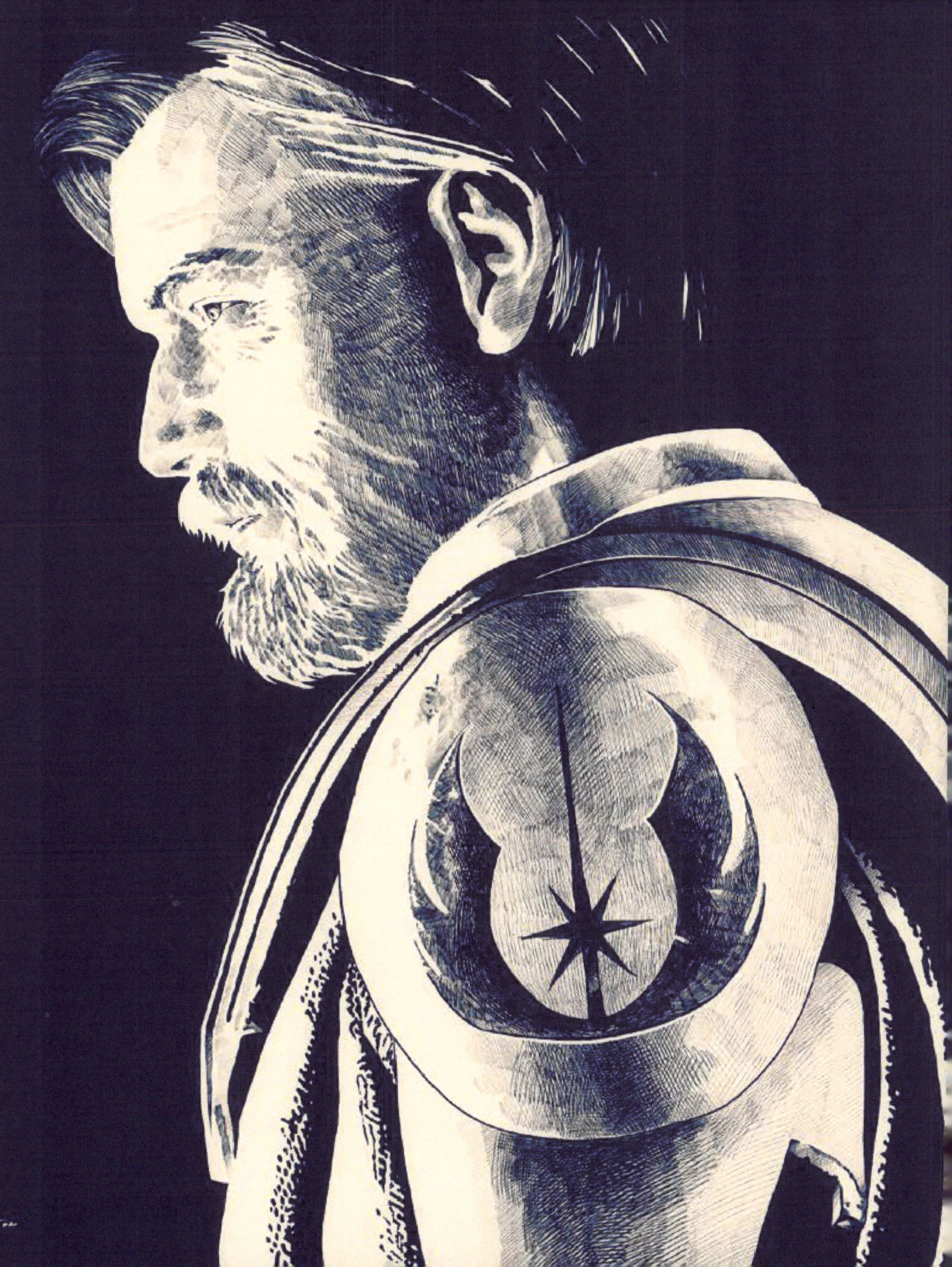

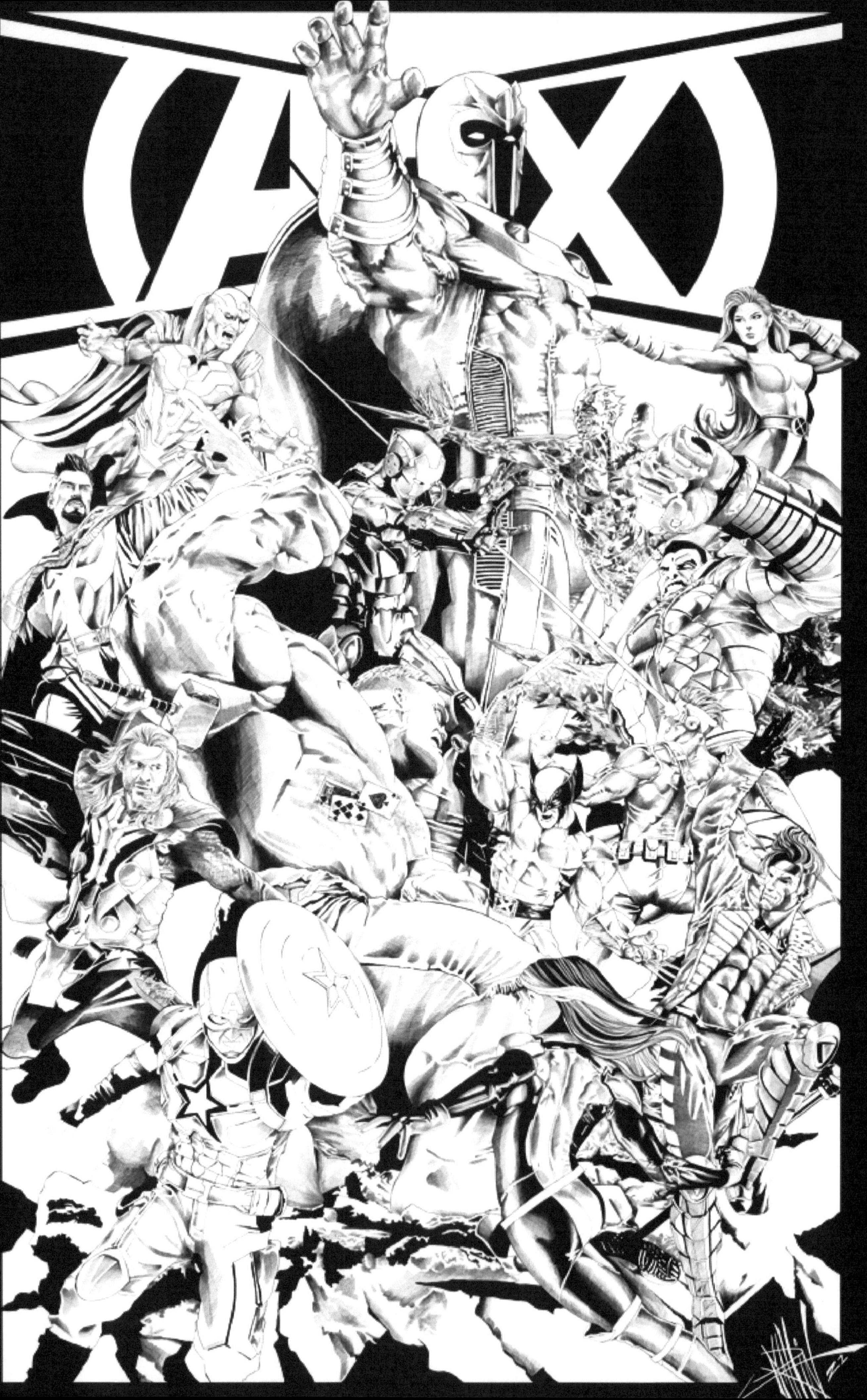

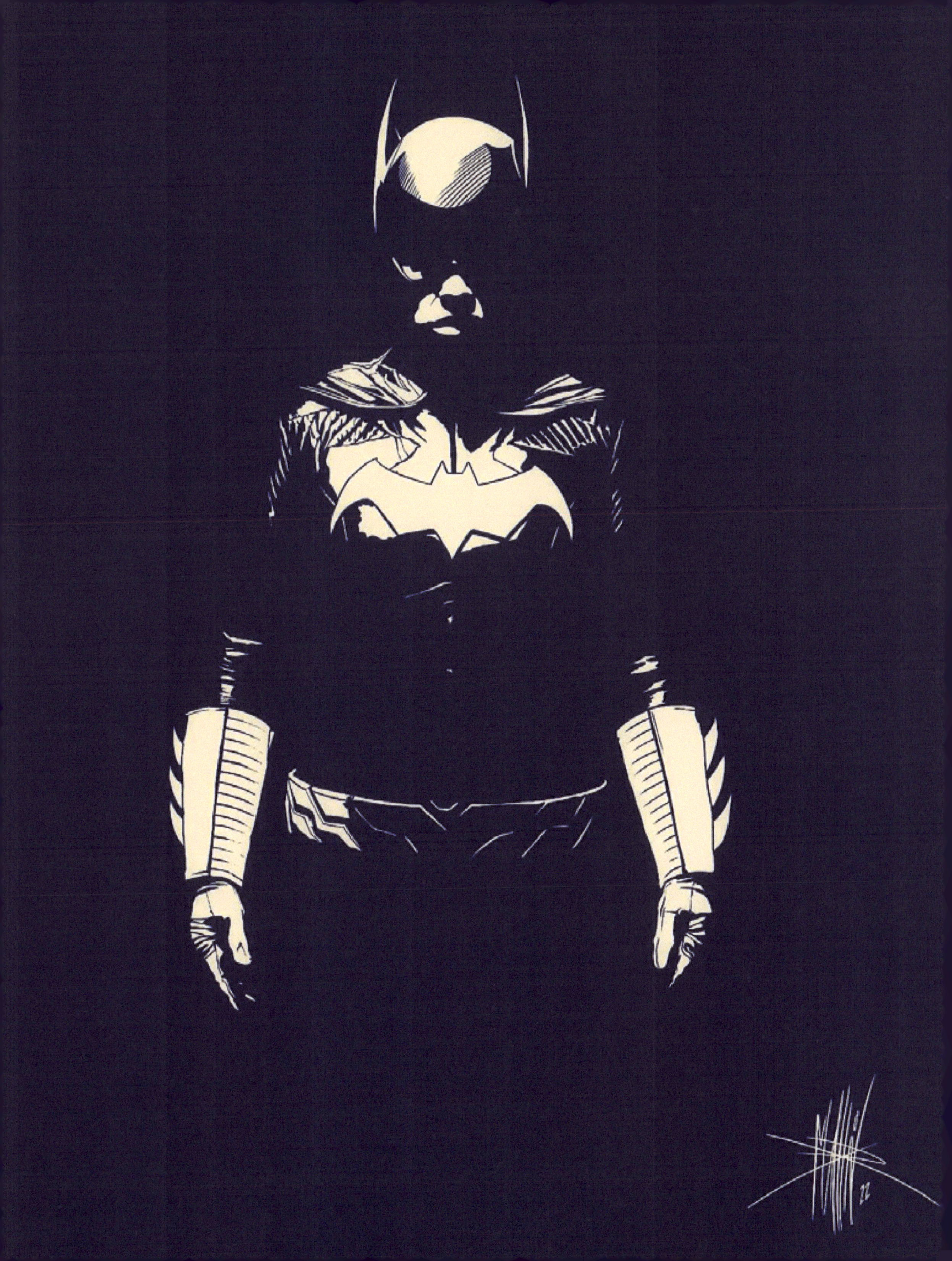

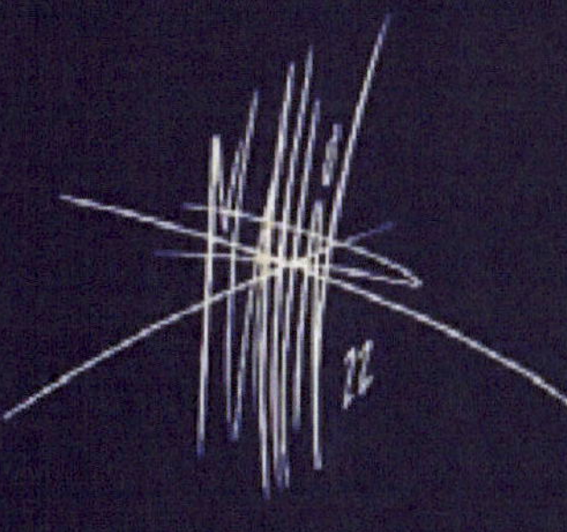

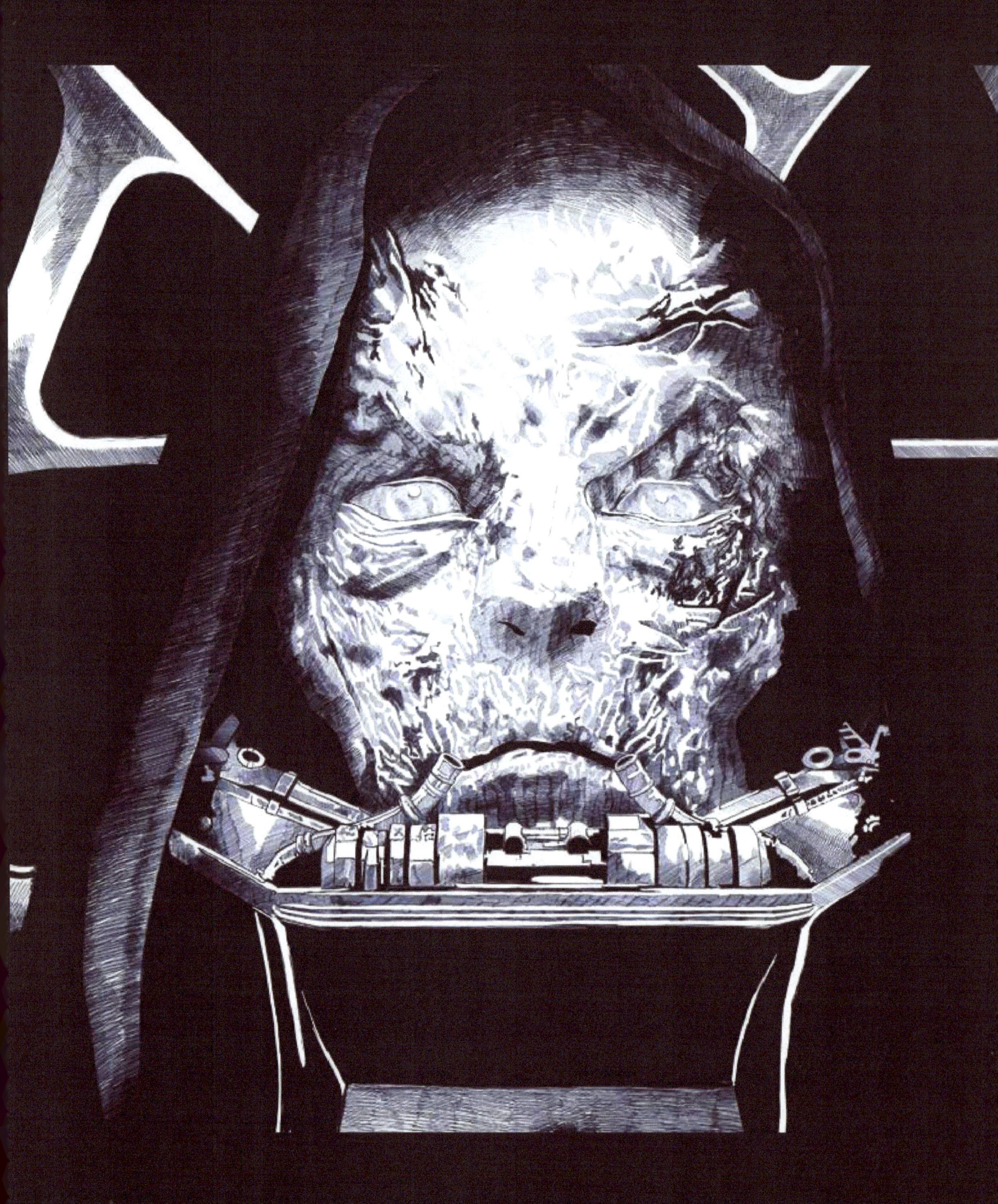

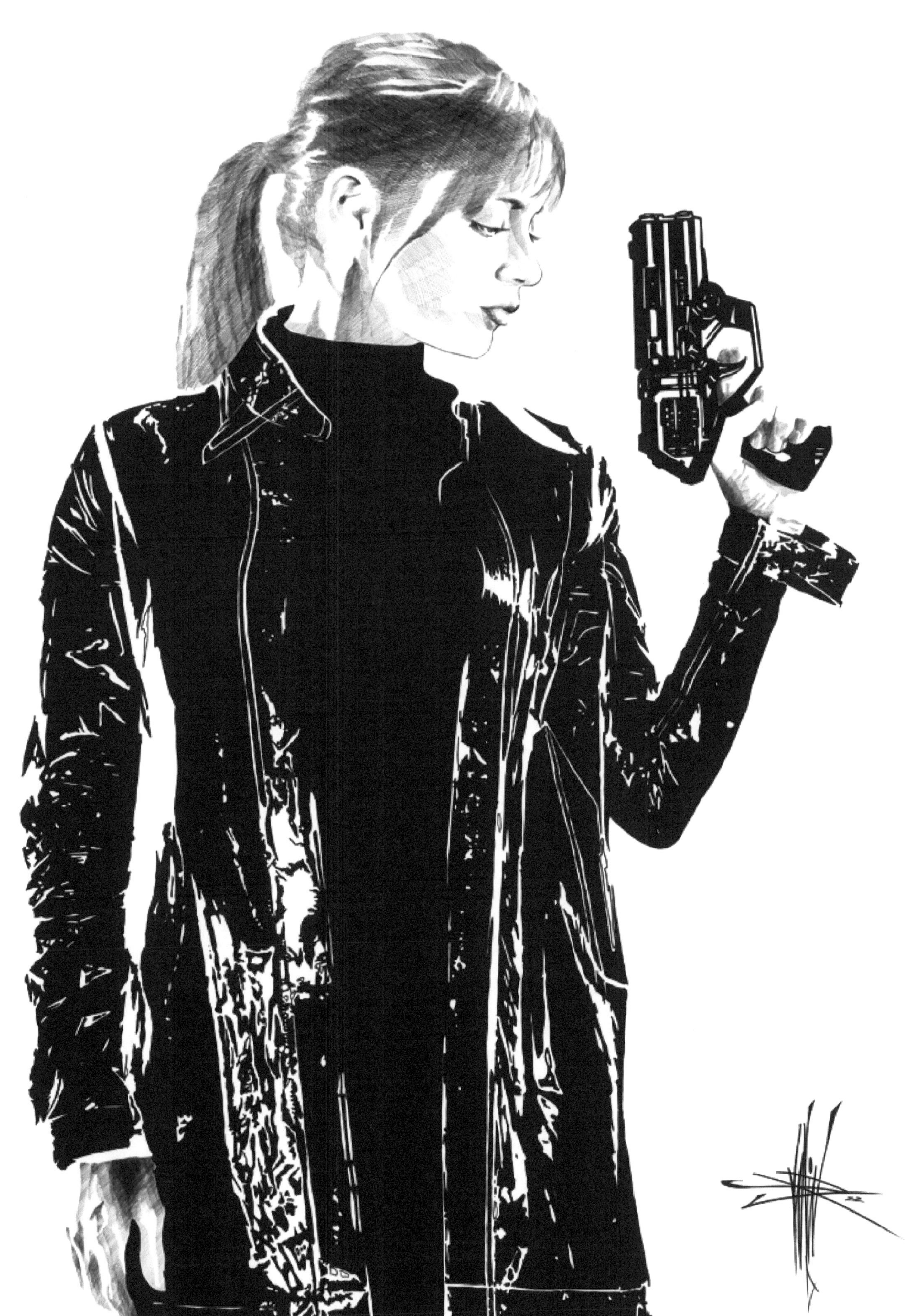

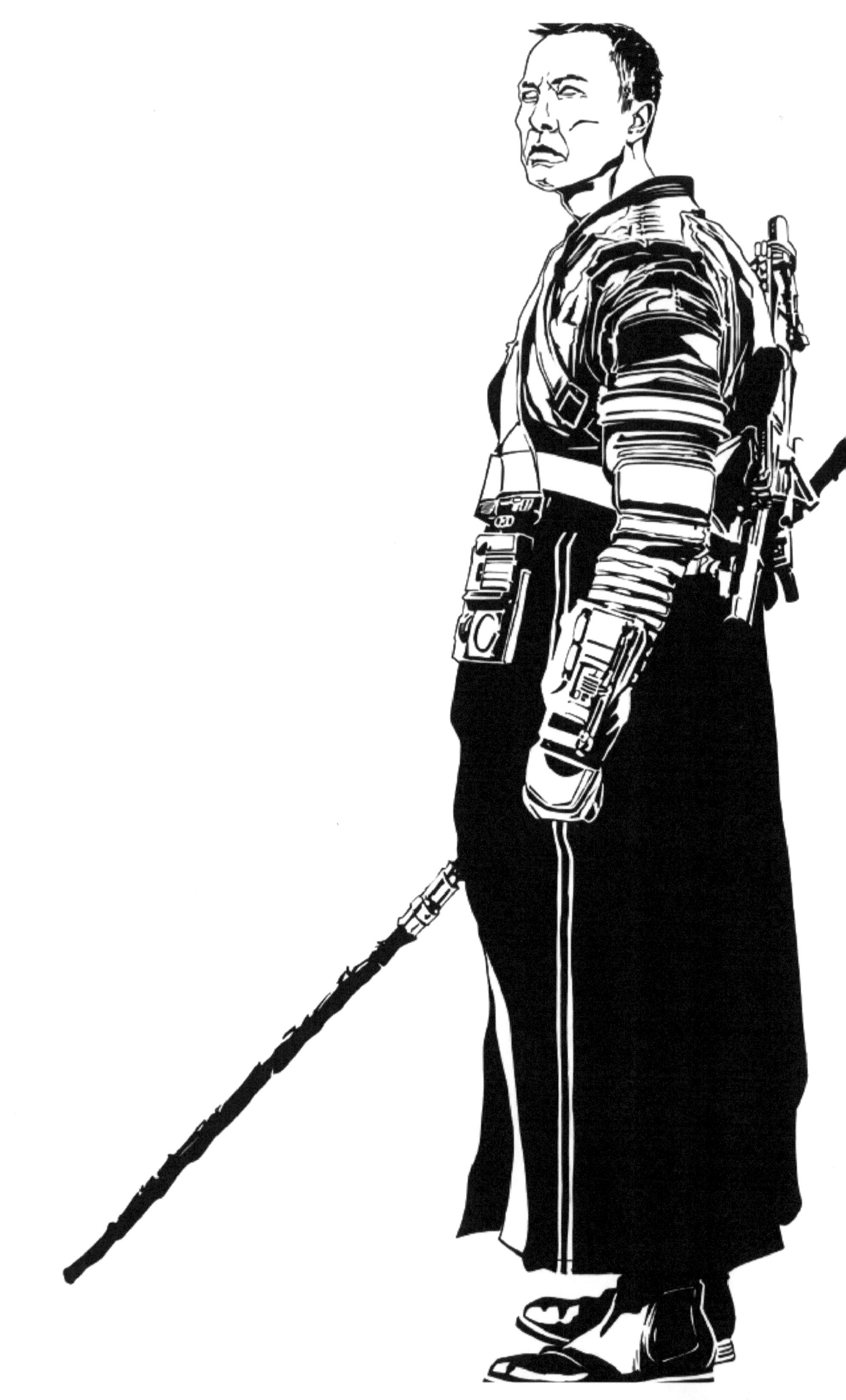

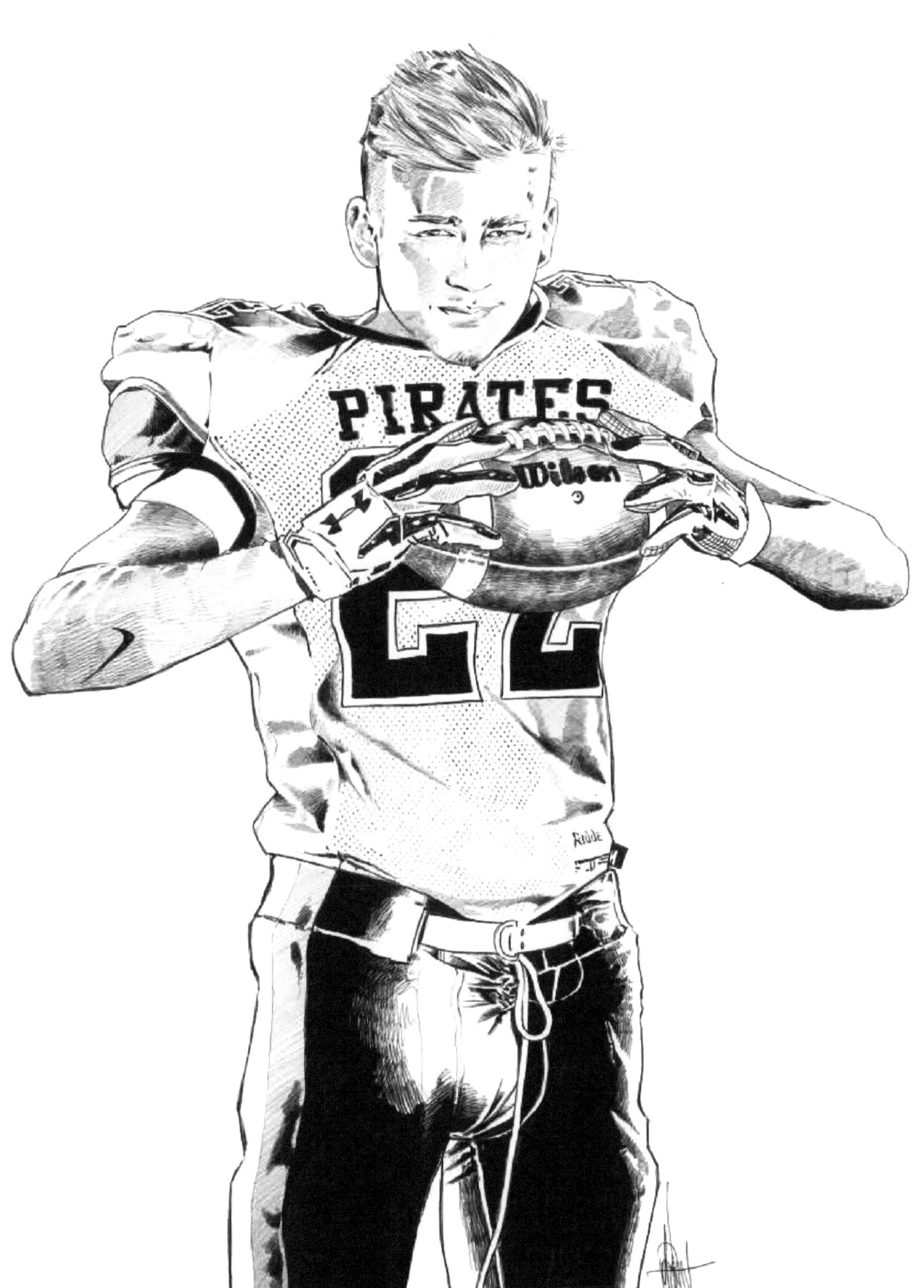

PIRATES
22
Wilson

WINS AND LOSSES COME A DIME A DOZEN. BUT
EFFORT? NOBODY CAN JUDGE THAT. BECAUSE EFFORT
IS BETWEEN YOU AND YOU.

RAY LEWIS

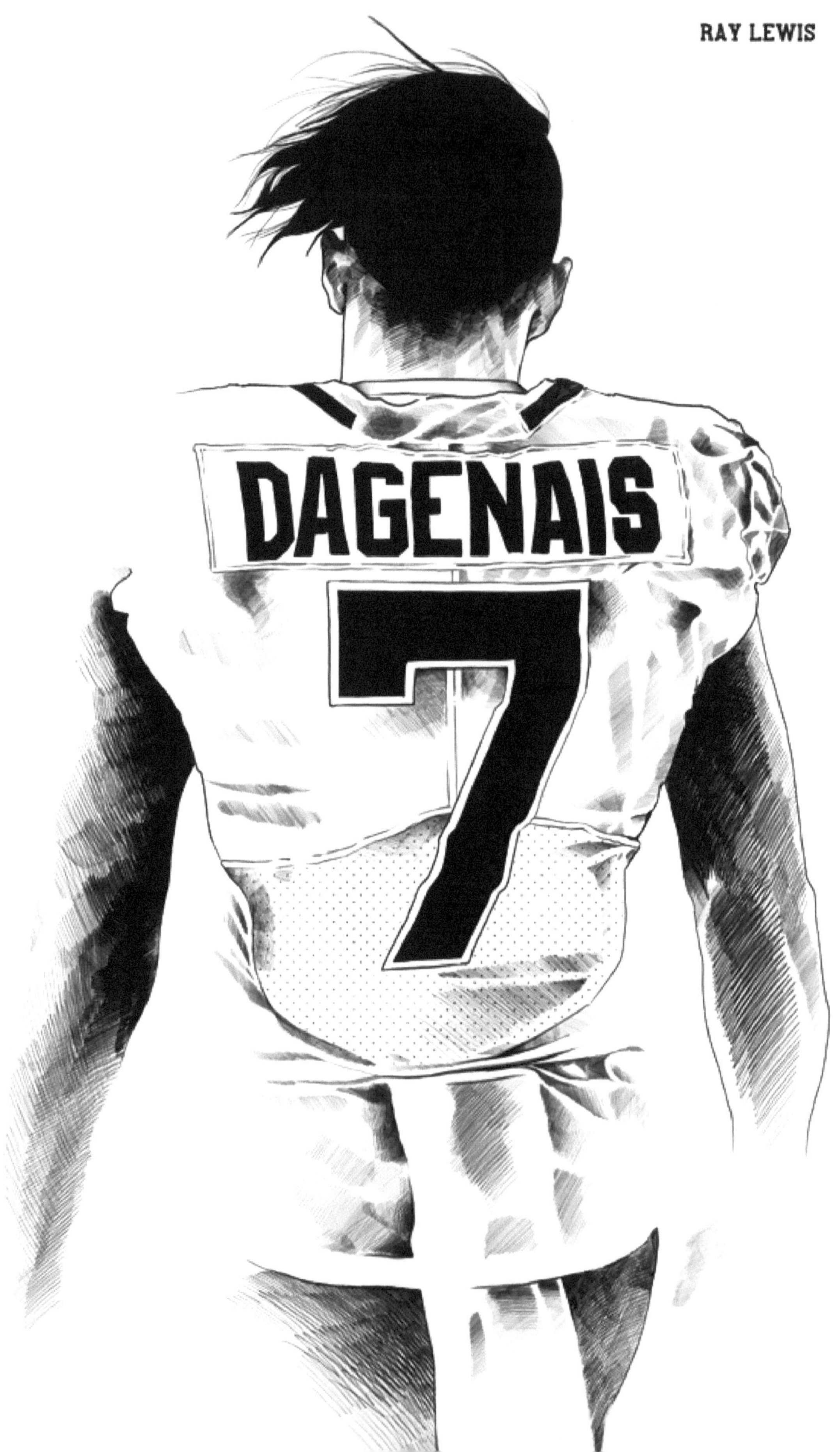
DAGENAIS
7

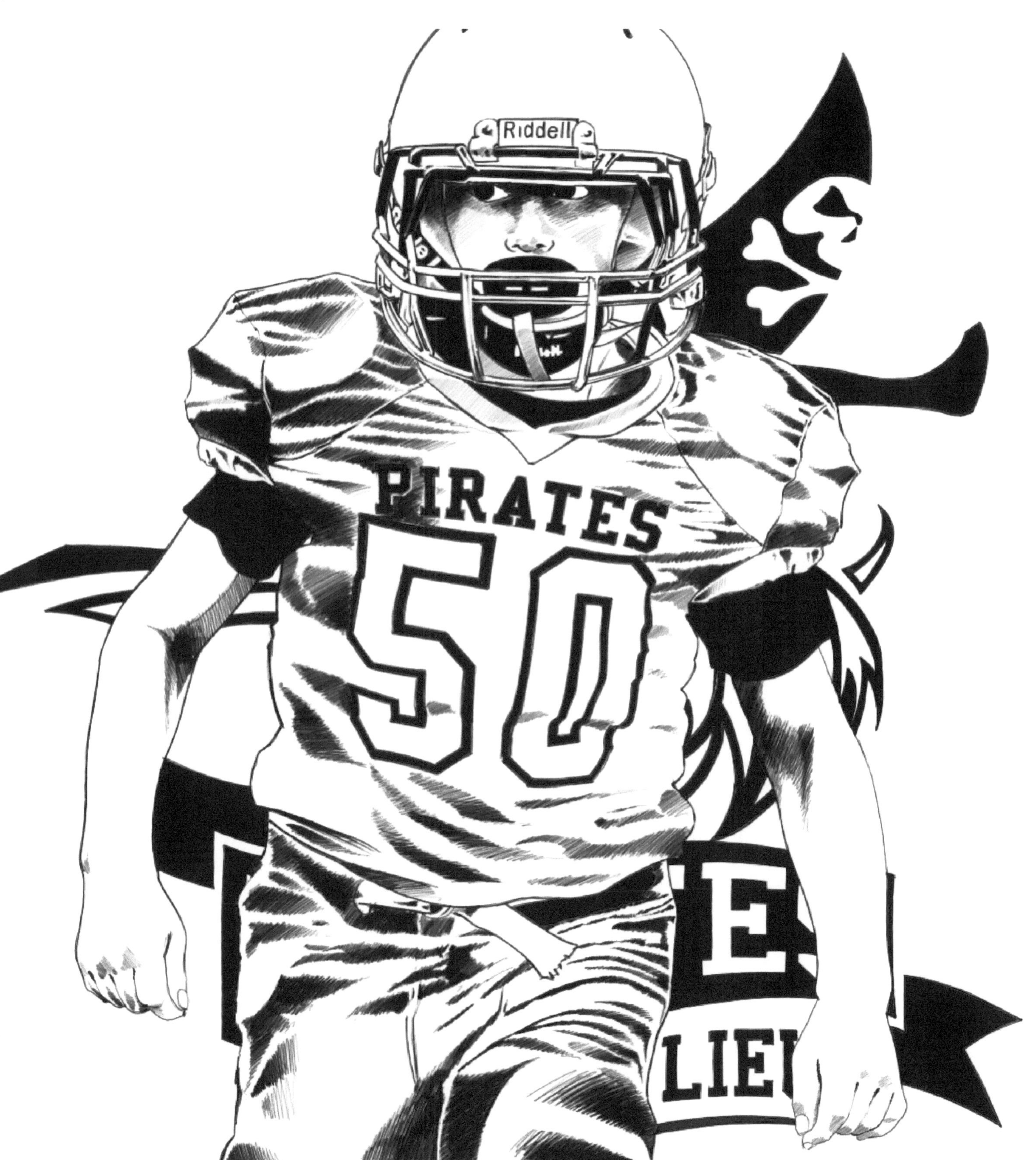
Riddell
PIRATES
50
E
LIE

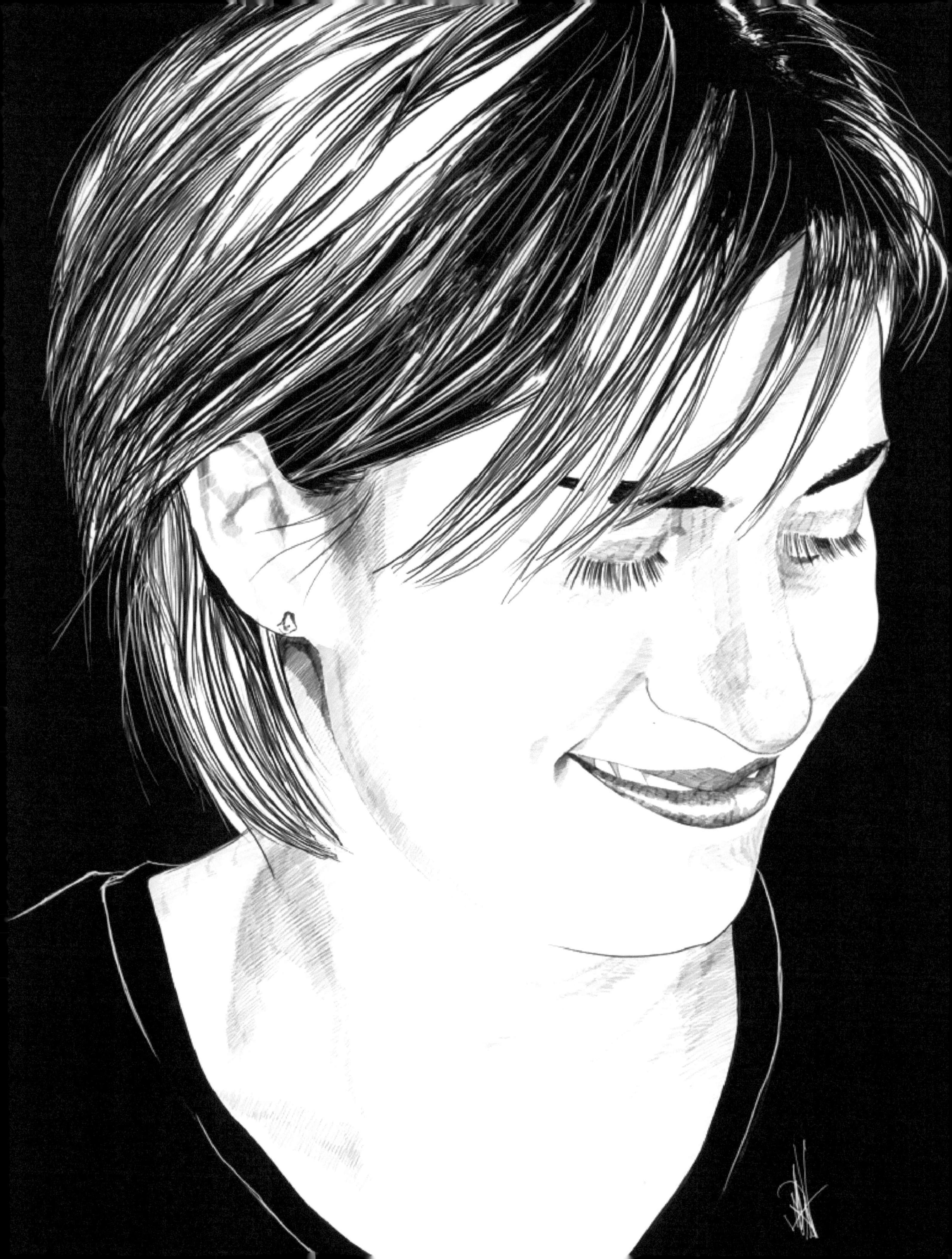

Acknowledgments

I want to thank my loving wife Debby Lyons for all the support you have given me during all these years. You always believed in me and for that, I will be forever grateful you are my muse.

I want to thank my brother Patrick Michel Dagenais who is himself an incredible photographer and artist. You made me want to be better.

I want to thank my mother Marie-Andrée LaPlante. You gave me my first shot with the logo for your dream. You made all this possible.

I want to thank children Gabriel Dagenais, Thomas Alexandre Dagenais, and Mikaël Dagenais who always made me feel like I was a superhero.

Lastly, I want to thank my father Guy Albert Dagenais. I wish you could see me now.

I love you all.

I also wanted to thank my friends in the comic book community who believed in me and supported my art during these past few years.

Kyle Goodman my partner in crime. Creator and writer of Here Walks Monsters

Noah Levesque from @noahsamazingreviews

Jeff from @hardtocomebuy

Bill Raupp from Grok Comics

Ross from Namesake Studios

Chris Fox @Wildcomics

Matthew Fox @mfstuntman

Efrain LaGuardia @passpoint_comics

Marvin Duran, Andy MacDonald, Tony Daniels, Dustin Rogers Bernard Chang, Jerry Ma, Nathan Birr, Daniel Kim, Alvaro Feliu Gutierrez, Sean Chen, Ken Knudtsen, Kala Sweets, and all the other artists from Battle of the Sketches

Legal Mentions

The following characters are a trademark of Marvel comics
Cyclops, Wolverine, Silver Surfer, Spider-Man, Spider-Man symbiote, Spider-Man noir, old men Spider-Man, Moon Night, Black Cat, the Human Torch, The Punisher, Electro, Red Sonja, Cable, Daredevil, Venom, Thor, Deadpool, Ghost Rider, Black Panther, Captain America, Ant-Man, Carnage, Ironfist, Thanos, Storm, Rogue, iceman, Colossus, Gambit, Jean Gray, Hulk, Vision, Dr Stange, Magneto, Ironman, the X-Men, The Avengers.
The following characters are a trademark of DC comics
Batman, Killer Croc, The Joker, Catwoman, Power Girl, The Laughing Batman, Nightwing, Bane, Batgirl, and Mr. Freeze.
The following characters are a trademark of The Walt Disney Company.
Tron, Starwars, Darth Vader, Boba Fett, General Kenobi, Ming-Na, Chirrut Îmwe.
Teenage Mutant Ninja Turtles is a trademark of VIACOM INTERNATIONAL INC.
Macross Plus is a trademark of Big West Co., Ltd.
Mazinger Z was created and is a trademark of Go Nagai.
SPAWN is a trademark of Todd McFarlane Productions.
LJN THUNDERCATS LION-O is a trademark of Warner Brothers Entertainment Inc.
Hellboy is a trademark of Dark Horse Comics.
Optimus Prime and Soundwave are trademarks of Hasbro.
Blade Runner is a trademark of Downhole Production Limited.
Creature From the Black Lagoon" is a trademark and copyright of Universal Studios.